ON THE COVER: In 1895 architect Fred Philip Fischer designed the Queen Anne-style home at 1723 Central Avenue, shown here on the far right, for lumberman George W. Scott. Alameda builder Denis Straub's company, D. Straub & Sons, executed Fischer's design, the sole survivor of a row of impressive homes that lined Central Avenue near Grand Street at the turn of the 19th to the 20th century. Straub and Fischer enjoyed an especially close relationship. In 1870 Straub married Fischer's mother, Louise Lauterwasser Fischer. Straub took Louise's eight children—Charles, Louisa, Annie, Kate, Fred Philip, Henry, John and Louis—into his heart and raised them as his own. Did you notice the bicycle on the curb in front of the Scotts' home?

Requests for permission or for further information should be addressed to:
Stellar Media Group, Inc.
3215 Encinal Avenue, Suite J
Alameda California 94501

ISBN: 978-1-60725-075-3

Printed in the United States of America

All photographs used with permission

Produced by Stellar Media Group, Inc.
Alameda, California

History is all around us

Alameda:
An Architectural Treasure Chest

Dennis Evanosky

Stellar Media Group, Inc.

TITLE PAGE PHOTO: August R. Denke Sr. waits to serve you behind the counter of his office in the Croll Building at Central Avenue and Webster Street. Denke was one of the more prolific architect-builders in Alameda, designing 35 homes and building 69. Like Denis Straub—whose stepson Fred Philip Fischer designed the home on our cover—Denke's sons were in the business: August R. Jr. worked as an architect and builder; Edward as an architect.

Table of Contents

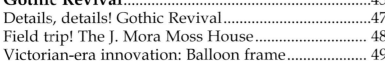

A heartfelt thank you

This book is decoration on a road already skillfully paved by four historians: Mark Wilson, Imelda Merlin, George Gunn and Woody Minor.

I first got to know Alameda in 1993 through a class I took with Mark Wilson. Mark's class included his book *East Bay Heritage: A Potpourri of Living History* with its architectural walking tours. Several of these tours included Alameda, and it was with Mark's book in hand that I first explored the Island City.

I stopped by the Alameda Museum along the way and met two more historians, one in print and the other in person. I purchased and studied Imelda Merlin's book *Alameda: A Geographical History*. Imelda's book covers much more than geography and enabled me to to begin to shape my own impressions of Alameda's history.

The other historian I met at the museum was its curator, George Gunn. George's two books *Documentation of Victorian and Post Victorian Residential and Commercial Buildings 1854 to 1904* and *Buildings of the Edwardian Period, City of Alameda 1905 to December 31, 1909* have proven to be extremely valuable resources. They are the only books I own two copies of: one for the car and one for home.

This pair of books contains complete and exhaustive lists of every home built in Alameda from its inception to 1910 and includes information about each home's style, architect, builder and first owner. I am especially indebted to George for taking so much time to answer my endless stream of questions about Alameda and its history.

The Alameda Museum also has a treasure trove of information with its collection of newspaper articles about Alameda. It was here that I first read Woody Minor's *Alameda Journal* articles. I would often visit the museum "for a little while" to read "a couple" of Woody's articles. I would end up spending hours reading, taking notes and then getting out the door to explore and photograph what I had learned from his articles and the exploration they led to.

It was these "Woody experiences" that led to my writing this book. I would like to thank *Alameda Journal* editor Connie Rux for granting me permission to quote from Woody's articles and, of course, Woody for researching and writing them.

Woody's contribution to recording Alameda's history does not stop with his *Alameda Journal* articles, however. His book *Taking Care of Business: Historic Commercial Buildings of the Island City* describes the development of Alameda's business districts and the history of Alameda's train and streetcar systems. I found this book especially helpful when it came time to describe A.A. Cohen's San Francisco & Alameda Railroad. I relied on another of Woody's books, *Alameda At Play*, for information about Lincoln, Longfellow and Woodstock parks. A special thanks goes to Alameda Recreation and Parks and Department director Dale Lillard for permission to quote from the book. Woody's information about the parks added spice to the hikes you'll find here.

Neither this nor my other books would have seen the light of day without help from my friends at Stellar Media Group, Inc. I was delighted when Eric J. Kos and Eric Turowski asked me to write some architectural history articles for the company's newspaper, the *Alameda Sun,* and its *Essence of Alameda* section. These articles are the heart and soul of the book you hold in your hands.

I would like to thank Julia Park Tracey, George Gunn and Eric J. Kos for lending me their proofreading skills. Their suggestions greatly improved this book. Its flaws are my own. A special thanks to Eric J. Kos for the maps he did for the "Take A Hike" sections.

The book reflects my interest in being able to identify and discuss architecture and its connection to history. I've attempted to pique your interest in Alameda's fascinating domestic architecture by expressing mine. I hope I've succeeded.

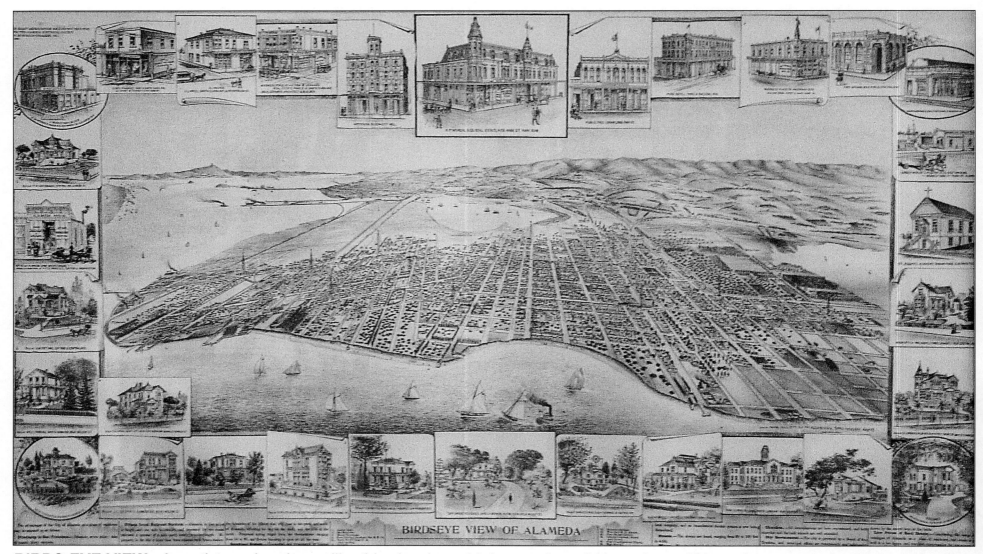

BIRDSEYE VIEW OF ALAMEDA

BIRDS-EYE VIEW: An artist-rendered map like this showing a birds-eye view of Alameda could have been yours for 25 cents (or five for just $1) in November 1887. The *Alameda Semi-Weekly Argus* commissioned the map for its readers. *Argus* editor Truman Daniels described how it was done: "The town was laid out in blocks on heavy paper with every attention paid (to) distance, perspective, etc. This the artist bends around a cardboard cylinder 8 to 10 inches in diameter. With this novel easel he travels around every block in the city filling in from actual observation on the map." Property owners who commissioned an individual view of their business block or residence paid $20 for a 3-inch by 3-inch drawing. Daniels was pleased. "We think the result is remarkably true to nature," the *Argus* editor proclaimed. Close-ups of this map are featured throughout this book.

Alameda's domestic architecture

Prologue: Defining an era

A rchitect Charles S. Shaner could design a home for you, but it would be expensive—$4,000 or more. We have a photo of Alameda paint dealer Eli B. Dunning proudly standing in front of the one Shaner designed for him for just that price. If $4,000 was too much for your taste, Peter Christiansen could build one for half that cost. And if you couldn't afford Peter's price, the firm of Marcuse & Remmel would get you into a comfortable home for just $1,650.

In an age when you can scarcely find a home on the Island for less than $400,000, it's a bit hard to believe upscale homes were available for $4,000, or that for as little as $1,650, you could have a home built from the ground up. That was another time, another era.

Queen Victoria reigned Great Britain from 1837 until 1901. Her monarchy defined the era when Dunning sold paint on Park Street. Architects and builders were dotting Alameda's landscape with homes we want to put under Her Majesty's umbrella and call "Victorian,"—but wait.

Mark Wilson teaches architectural history and has written what I consider the definitive work about the area's 19th century architecture, *A Living Legacy: Historic Architecture of the East Bay*. His

ELI B. DUNNING stands in front of the Santa Clara Avenue home where he lived with his wife, Sarah. From the finial on the porch gable to the Eastlake sunburst on the upstairs gable, the home has many of the trappings of the Queen Anne style.

book includes an Alameda chapter with several walking tours of Island City neighborhoods. In his lectures, Wilson is quick to point out that there is no such thing as Victorian architecture; there is only Victorian-*era* architecture.

Oakland's Pardee Home Museum curator David Nicolai begins his tours by asking his audience to define the style of the 1868 home. He waits a few moments before he adds with a smile, "And don't say Victorian."

He waits again in the silence that has overtaken the stunned group. They were all so sure, so ready to enthusiastically reply, "Victorian."

Nicolai then points out that the Pardee Home is not a Victorian home, but a *Victorian-era* home in the Italianate style. We will see some fine examples of this Victorian-era style here in Alameda.

The first two Victorian-era styles, Greek and Gothic Revival, were survivors that architects developed before Victoria's coronation on June 20, 1837. Greek Revival arrived in the United States when Benjamin Latrobe designed the Bank of Pennsylvania building in 1803. Latrobe's greatest contribution to our architecture, however, came to pass at the bidding of President Thomas Jefferson. Latrobe designed the United States Capitol.

We can easily dispense with Greek Revival; those who settled here in the 19th century did not use this style for residential architecture. A stately Greek Revival survivor stands as the Benicia State Capitol building. Our first field trip will take us there. Elements of the style survived, though; architects used them extensively in the Italianate and Classical Revival styles.

Scholars often cite Alexander Jackson Davis' 1838 Gothic Revival creation, "Lyndhurst" in Tarrytown, New York, as one of the style's early appearances in this country.

Just before the middle of the 19th century, industrialism—and the machinery it created—allowed a more complicated and elaborate architecture. Prominent styles during Victoria's reign include

ALBERT A. HIBBARD moved into this Clinton Avenue Queen Anne house when it was brand new in 1892. That may be Albert's children Geraldine and Southerland standing in front of the home.

Italianate, Second Empire, Stick and Queen Anne. We'll look at each in turn.

Architectural inspiration did not come to a halt with Queen Victoria's death on February 22, 1901, however. The world had turned a corner a year earlier and entered the 20th century. Other styles had already taken the stage, including Craftsman and Colonial Revival. Still other revival styles appeared on the landscape after World War I: Mediterranean and Tudor Revival, for example. Then came a type of home that builders could dress in any style—the bungalow.

Homes dressed in these styles are best understood in their historical context. So first we'll take a closer look at Alameda's early history. This will give us a better understanding of the styles and how they evolved.

Let's get started with a field trip to Benicia to have a look at the earliest of the Victorian-era styles, Greek Revival.

Early American architecture utilized Classical elements in its design. The Federal style took its inspiration from the British habit of embellishing their buildings with garlands, swags and Palladian windows.

The War of 1812 soured relations between the United States and England, and Americans looked elsewhere for inspiration. They found it in Greece, where a revolution not unlike their own took place in 1820.

American architects began to imitate Greek temples with their massive entryway columns, front-facing gables and oversized front doors. Public buildings arose in this new style, most notably the construction of the rotunda on the United States Capitol begun in 1826. (The British had partially destroyed the building during the War of 1812.)

Many plantation owners in the South built homes in the Greek Revival style. It did not catch on in other parts of the country as a domestic style, however. Early

THIS STATELY BRICK EDIFICE in Benicia housed California's third seat of government (the previous two were at San Jose and Vallejo). The Greek Revival building—the only surviving pre-Sacramento capitol—served as the capitol of California from February 11, 1853 to February 28, 1854.

Californians decided to use the Greek Revival style when they built their capitol in Benicia in 1852.

By the time European settlers arrived in Alameda, the Greek Revival style had given way to Gothic Revival.

Some 40 years later, in 1893 Chicago's Columbian Exposition showcased Classical buildings and sparked a renewed interest in the Greek Revival style.

Field trip!

A Greek Revival survivor

Benicia State Capitol
115 West G Street
Benicia, CA 94510

(707) 745-3385
It's always wise to call ahead and check opening times before embarking on a field trip.

One of the prettiest examples of a building in this late 19th- and early 20th-century re-awakening is right here in Alameda—the 1904 First Presbyterian Church at Santa Clara Avenue and Chestnut Street. Stop by and have a look. If you do, notice the Corinthian columns graced with acanthus leaves and the front-facing gable that resembles the one on the Capitol in Benicia.

CULTURE CLASH: When the City of Alameda extended Santa Clara Avenue through the heart of the old Sather Mound in 1908, workers found remnants of a past culture. Notice the man on the left contemplating a skull; that's the amatuer anthropologist Captain Clark, who led the excavation. A young man displays a pair of "crossbones" nearby.

 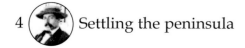

Part One

Settling the peninsula

The first inhabitants

Today's Island City began life as a peninsula where Native Americans first lived more than 3,000 years ago. These first settlers took advantage of the climate and the readily available staples—acorns, game, fresh water and oysters. They left shell mounds as their legacy, but nothing of these remains today. The largest of these mounds took on the name of the family who owned the property where the mound was located. It's a name familiar to most of us.

When you mention the name "Sather" to most locals, the Sather Gate and the Sather Tower on the University of California, Berkeley campus might come immediately to mind. The university's Sather Chair in History and the Sather Professorship of Classical Literature might also jog the memory bank. Bring the "Sather Mound" in Alameda into a conversation, however, and most brows immediately furrow.

How did the name Sather come to be associated with a long-disappeared mound of oyster shells?

A HIKE AROUND the site of the Sather Mound would not be complete without a visit to the Alameda Museum, where these relics, which were found in the mound, are exhibited.

Peder Sather was born in the city of Trondhjem on Norway's north-central coast on September 17, 1810. He worked as a fisherman until he was 30 years old. He then decided to emigrate to the United States. He arrived in New York in 1841; nine years later he went west.

In 1850 he and Edward W. Church opened a bank. The enterprising pair saw the advantage of meeting arriving ships before their passengers could even get ashore. To that end, they built in a wooden shanty on piles over San Francisco Bay. Their venture grew into the banking office, "Sather & Church."

The 1860 federal census tells us that the prosperous pair was living across the bay in Alameda with their families. They likely kept two households each, one on San Francisco's Rincon Hill and a second on the sunnier peninsula on the *contra costa*.

The census tells us that Peder lived in Alameda with his first wife, Sarah, and their four children: daughters Caroline, Josephine and Mary and son, Peder. Among the properties

Peder Sather purchased on and near the peninsula were two tracts of land, one to the west of the Town of Alameda, the other to the north. This second tract contained a mound that Native Americans had taken thousands of years to build (and that newcomers would take about 50 years to obliterate.)

By the time the Sathers arrived, enterprising Yankees—including the town's founders, William Worthington Chipman and Gideon Aughinbaugh—had already begun shaving the mound down to size.

They carted soil away to help cultivate their gardens and orchards. Then they went to work on the shells and human remains, using this macabre mix to pave roads on each end of the peninsula.

The Native American presence was especially concentrated in the peninsula's eastern half, Imelda Merlin tells us in *Alameda: A Geographical History*. "Four mounds were found east of Park Street and two others between Park and Chestnut streets," she says.

The largest mound measured 400 feet by 100 feet and was 14 feet high at its apex. A nearby spring provided fresh water, and no doubt attracted the Native Americans to the site.

Three other factors made the site particularly attractive:
- Proximity of a fresh-water creek that we know as Sausal Creek
- Ponds that provided tule branches for constructing boats and houses
- Oyster beds just offshore in the bay.

The arrival of the Europeans spelled an end to Native American culture. First the Spanish set out to convert the Indians to Christianity. In order to better control the indigenous peoples, soldiers and padres herded them onto mission property, "properly clothed" them and treated them as little more than slaves. The Indians whom the Spanish did not capture or kill fled inland.

Then the Yankees arrived. By then, few, if any, Native Americans were present to witness the destruction of a culture that included the shell mounds that had existed on today's Alameda; sacred remains the newcomers turned into topsoil and road beds.

WHEN WORKERS excavated the Sather Mound in 1908, they found artifacts like these tools and jewelry that are now on display at the Alameda Museum.

 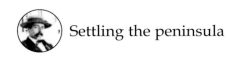

Take a hike!

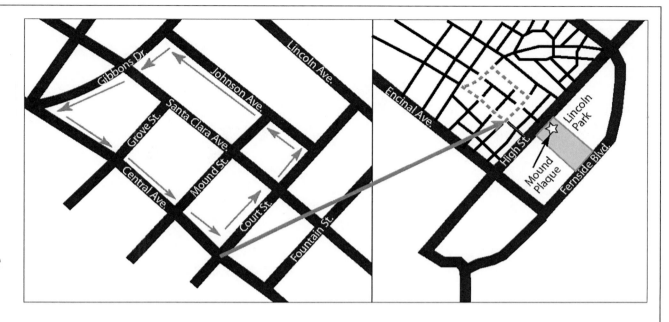

Stroll around the Sather Mound

In order to best appreciate the Sather Mound, strap on your walking shoes and walk its perimeter. As you start, try to imagine a landscape full of oak trees. Listen for what the Ohlone may have heard: the music of water flowing from a nearby spring, racing down the creek bed just to the north and lapping the shores of the bay to the south and east.

Start at Central Avenue and Court Street and walk north to Johnson Avenue. When you cross Santa Clara Avenue, look up and down the street. Santa Clara was cut through the remnants of the mound in 1908. The especially telling photograph, shown on page 4, taken somewhere along the avenue here shows workers posing for the camera. This shows us how little respect early 20th century Alamedans paid to the Native American presence.

Walk west on Johnson Avenue to Gibbons Drive. Here you would be just alongside the mound. Look up and imagine a "hill" 14 feet high and bigger than a football field and you'll appreciate the size of this creation.

This was a sacred place, where the Native Americans buried their dead—450 bodies were removed from the mound. Merlin says they were all lying on their sides facing the rising sun with arms and feet drawn up.

Continue your walk up Gibbons to Central Avenue; then walk down Central back to Court Street. If you have time, walk back down Santa Clara Avenue to Lincoln Park and have a look at the plaque inside the park. The Daughters of the American Revolution erected it in 1914 to commemorate the Sather Mound. And if you visit the Alameda Museum, you'll see some of the artifacts found in the mound.

JULIO

HIDES AND TALLOW were the mainstays of the economy the Spanish brought north from today's Mexico. A panel on a mural at Peralta Hacienda Park depicts workers making tallow and pouring the product into bags made of hides. To keep his livestock from roaming onto the property he sold to the Yankees, Don Antonio Peralta required William W. Chipman and Gideon Aughinbaugh to build a fence at the border of his property and the *Bolsa de Encinal*.

European pioneers

Don Antonio Peralta's *Bolsa de Encinal*

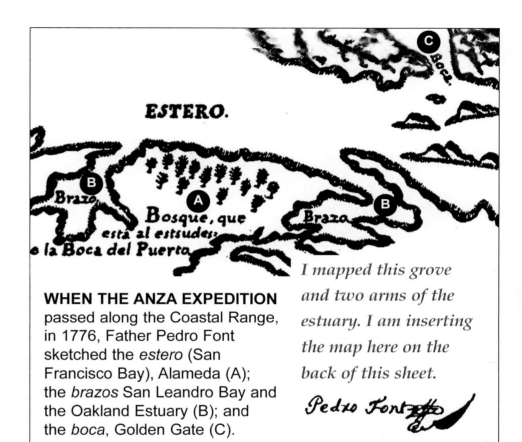

WHEN THE ANZA EXPEDITION passed along the Coastal Range, in 1776, Father Pedro Font sketched the *estero* (San Francisco Bay), Alameda (A); the *brazos* San Leandro Bay and the Oakland Estuary (B); and the *boca*, Golden Gate (C).

I mapped this grove and two arms of the estuary. I am inserting the map here on the back of this sheet.

Pedro Font

W hen the Spanish trekked through today's East Bay in 1770 and again in 1772 they paid no attention to the peninsula that is today's Alameda.

On April 1, 1776, as the members of the Anza Expedition paused in the hills just above today's Leona Heights in Oakland, Father Pedro Font took advantage of the break and opened his diary. "I mapped this grove and two arms of the estuary," Font wrote in his diary. "I am inserting the map here on the back of this sheet." Font sketched a grove of trees on the peninsula and labeled the grove, *"Bosque que esta al estsudeste de la Boca del Puerte"* (the woodland that is east-southeast of the mouth of the port.) He included the *"boca,"* (mouth), today's Golden Gate, on his hastily sketched map. He also drew a pair of watery *"brazos"* (arms) embracing the woodland. We know these arms as today's San Leandro Bay and Oakland Estuary. Font's "woodland" became modern-day Alameda and parts of Oakland.

Thanks to Father Pedro Font and his diary, we have the first map of Alameda. Seventeen-year-old Luis Maria Peralta may have heard of, or even seen, this map. Luis had accompanied his parents and siblings on the Anza Expedition. He could not realize then that 46 years later, he would own almost all he surveyed on this side of the *"estero,"* the strait, as Font called San Francisco Bay on his map.

The Spanish and other early settlers later called Font's woodland the *"Bolsa de Encinal"* (Purse of Oak Groves) because its geography reminded them of a purse.

Font's woodland also took the name *"Encinal de San Antonio"* (Saint Anthony's Oak Grove). When Spanish explorer and mapmaker Jose de Canizares mapped San Francisco Bay in 1776, he

DON ANTONIO PERALTA joined his three brothers in tending his father's, (Luis Maria Peralta), 35-square-mile estate. In 1844 Luis deeded 15,206 acres to Antonio. The deed included the *Bolsa de Encinal,* today's Alameda.

used only one label for all of today's East Bay: *"Punta de San Antonio"* (Saint Anthony's Point). The *Encinal de San Antonio,* San Antonio Creek—the name the early settlers gave the Oakland Estuary—and the Peralta's *Rancho de San Antonio* likely took their names from Canizares' label.

In 1820, the King of Spain rewarded Luis Peralta for his faithful military service with a boon that would make any veteran smile: 44,500 choice acres across the bay from the Presidio. The grant encompassed most of the region we call the East Bay, including the *Bolsa de Encinal.*

Don Luis chose to live in San Jose and gave his four sons, Ignacio, Domingo, Vicente and Antonio the task of managing his vast estate. In 1844, he assigned the area that contained Font's woodland to his youngest son, Antonio. Four years later Don Antonio learned of Peter Parfait's presence on the *Bolsa.* The don granted the Belgian and his Native American wife permission to keep a garden and cut firewood for their own use. He also allowed them to harvest game and livestock for their personal consumption.

In 1850 Joseph Depassier and Jose Maria Payot met with Antonio, who granted the pair a 6-year lease to the entire penin-

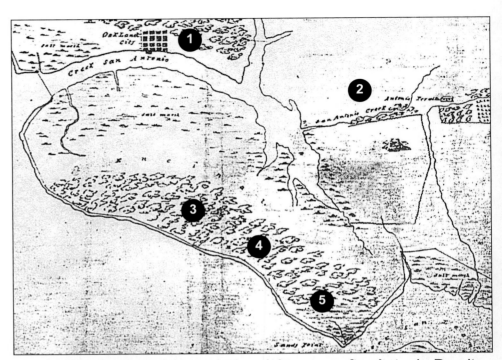

THIS MAP WAS MADE in 1852—eight years after Antonio Peralta took possession of the land that included the *Bolsa de Encinal.* By then Horace Moon, Edson Adams and Horace Carpentier had laid out the city of Oakland (1). The map included Peralta's 1821 hacienda (2), but failed to point out the *Bolsa's* early residents like Joseph Depassier and Balthazar Maitre (3), Peter Parfait and his Native American wife (4) and Stephen and Daniel Salmon (5.) The 1852 California census lists others living on the peninsula as well.

sula. The following year, Payot transferred his interest in the lease to Balthazar Maitre. By then William Worthington Chipman and Gideon Aughinbaugh had visited Depassier and Maitre. They leased 160 acres from them and expressed their desire to buy the entire *Bolsa de Encinal.* The Frenchmen weren't worried, though. They knew Don Antonio disliked the Yankees; he would never sell.

The Yankees arrive

Yankees. Joseph Depassier and Balthazar Maitre were right. Don Antonio Peralta had little use for these newcomers, and the Don viewed the pair across the table from him as Yankees in the truest sense of the word: They had recently arrived from from the east, and they wanted his land. These two men surprised the Don, however.

Rather than having to answer to him what they were doing on his property, William Worthington Chipman and Gideon Aughinbaugh had politely come to him and explained they had leased 160 acres from his tenants, Depassier and Maitre.

Chipman told Peralta that he was looking for a change. His partner in an "intelligence bureau" across the bay had decided to move to Sacramento. Aughinbaugh had little to say. He and his wife, Elizabeth, owned a grocery store at First and Mission streets in San Francisco; he wanted as little discussion as possible about the value of the fruit they were raising in their new orchards. The pair told the Don they would like to purchase his entire *Bolsa de Encinal*. When Don Antonio reminded them he already had   tenants, Chipman and Aughinbaugh promised

SPLITTING UP THE PIE: This map shows how W. W. Chipman and Gideon Aughinbaugh kept part of the peninsula for themselves (A). They sold portions to other enterprising newcomers Henry Fitch and William Sharon (B); Charles Hibbard (C); James Foley (D); former Texas Rangers Jack Hays and John Caperton (E). They later sold the peninsula's West End to Charles Bowman (F).

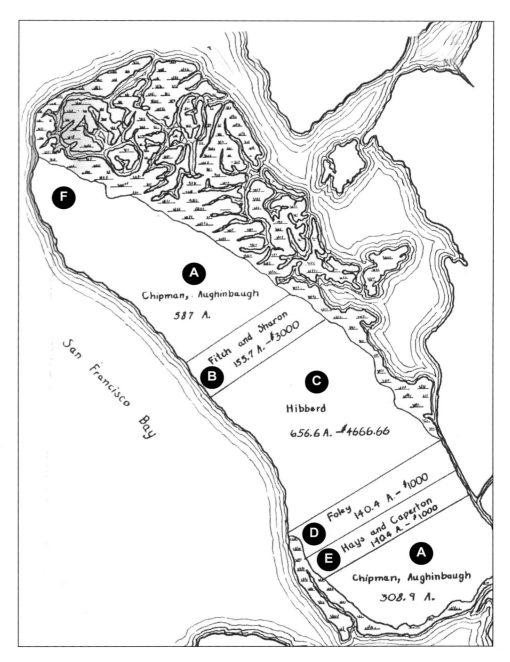

San Francisco Bay

Chipman, Aughinbaugh 587 A.

Fitch and Sharon 155.7 A. – $3000

Hibbard 656.6 A. – $4666.66

Foley 140.4 A. – $1000

Hays and Caperton 140.4 A. – $1000

Chipman, Aughinbaugh 308.9 A.

him they would honor the lease he had with Depassier and Maitre until it expired in 1856. They also promised Don Antonio they would leave Peter Parfait and his wife in peace.

Chipman and Aughinbaugh politely explained to the Don that they were more than just a pair of Yankees interested in his land. They told him they wanted to build a town; maybe name it for the Peralta family.

So, in October 1851, the Don sold the *Bolsa de Encinal* to this pair of enterprising Yankees for $14,000. To seal the deal, Don Antonio insisted on $2,000 when they inked the deed with a promise of $5,000 one week later and the balance of $7,000 due

CHARCOAL MAKERS: Depassier and Maitre lived in this home that they had barged across San Francisco Bay and re-built at the site of today's 1816 San Jose Avenue, near Chestnut Street and San Jose Avenue. The pair made charcoal, which was widely used to purify water.

within a year. The new property owners borrowed $5,000 from Samuel King and $5,000 from the bank. They likely paid the balance out of their own pockets. To raise the $10,000 to repay King and the bank, Chipman and Aughinbaugh sold 1,023.1 of the peninsula's 1,919 acres to investors for a grand total of $9,666.66, keeping 895.9 acres for themselves. This included:

- 656.6 acres to Charles Hibbard for $4,666.66
- 157.7 acres to Henry Fitch and William Sharon for $3,000
- 104.4 acres to Jack Hays, J. J. McMurtry and John Caperton for $1,000
- 104.4 acres to J. J. Foley for $1,000

After Chipman and Aughinbaugh deeded 144 acres of their net 895.9 acres at the peninsula's western tip to Charles C. Bowman, they were left with 751.9 acres in two parcels—one at the western end, the other at the eastern end of the peninsula.

Counting heads

The first federal census in California was taken in 1850. In an unfortunate turn of events, records for Contra Costa and Santa Clara counties were lost; fire destroyed the San Francisco records. (Alameda County did not exist in 1850. It was created April 6, 1853, from parts of Contra Costa and Santa Clara counties.)

The men who drafted California's constitution in 1849 had unknowingly provided a solution to the problem of lost and burned records. Article IV read in part, "a census is required to be taken in 1852, in 1855 and every 10 years thereafter."

Census taker Samuel Tennant arrived on the peninsula in September 1852—almost a year after Chipman and Aughinbaugh had purchased it from Antonio Peralta. There he met and duly recorded 44 inhabitants. He included the founders of the new Town of Alameda listing names, ages and gender as "Chipman, W. W., 21 (he was 32!), M" and "Aughinbaugh, G., 36, M."

Tennant also listed William's brother Edward as "Chipman, E. S., 31" and Gideon's wife and daughter as "Aughinbaugh, Edith, 26, F" and "Aughinbaugh, E. A., 4, F."

Among the other inhabitants Tennant enumerated German native John Fish and Frenchmen Francis Souleran, Constant Batterout, August Loraine and Antonio Orosco. All these men told Tennant they were laborers.

The census taker also recorded a pair of brickmakers: Frenchmen Jean Moulini and Isadore Guerin; a French cook, Bonnie Archil; and 10 inhabitants who gave their professions as "farmers." These farmers included the Chipman brothers, William and Edward; the Salmon brothers, Stephen and Daniel, and Wisconsin native Julius Chester. The most intriguing entry on Tennant's pages was Chilean native Ariste Dangeroo, who gave his profession as "overseer."

New town reflects new county

Just one month after the creation of Alameda County, Chipman and Aughinbaugh laid out the Town of Alameda. I'd like to speculate that they named their town for the new county. They had hopes of attracting the county seat. The founders threw their hats in the ring, and on December 5, 1854, Alameda Township received 232 of 2,368 votes cast to become county seat. (Oakland received just 11 votes; San Leandro emerged the winner with 732 votes.)

By 1864, the peninsula had become home to three separate towns: Alameda on the eastern shore, Woodstock on the western shore and Encinal in between. A.A. Cohen built the San Francisco & Alameda Railroad that same year. Then, on September 6, 1869, the transcontinental railroad arrived on Cohen's rail line, and, for a little while, the peninsula's town of Woodstock served as the terminus for the transcontinental railroad.

Let's explore the towns before we look at the architectural styles that defined the peninsula.

Pesky squatters

Squatters were so prevalent in Contra Costa County—where the Alameda peninsula was located until the creation of Alameda County in 1853—that the 1852 California census listed only three towns: Martinez, Oakland and "Squattersville."

When California first became a state in 1850, the United States government allowed people to "squat" on unclaimed land. Anyone who improved the property could claim it as his own. The land that contained "Squattersville," however, was not unclaimed. It belonged to Francisco Soto and Jose Estudillo, who spent time (and money) in the courts to force the newcomers to either buy the land or leave. ("Squattersville" later became San Lorenzo.)

Don Antonio Peralta was the first, but would by no means be the last, property owner to worry about squatters on the *Bolsa de Encinal*. W. W. Chipman, Gideon Aughinbaugh and James J. Foley would also deplete resources fighting the illegal claims of squatters on their properties, often just giving in to them. Chipman detested the squatters, calling them "knights errant"; he referred to two of them pointedly as "Squatter Jones" and "Squatter Matthews" in his diary. Foley handed Franklin Pancoast and Julius Chester five acres each to get the squatting pair off his back.

Henry Fitch and William Sharon conveyed the property they had purchased from Chipman and Aughinbaugh to Charles L. Fitch in 1854. Charles took possession three years later and held the property by force of arms. It seems the Squatter's League was helping uninvited guests onto his land.

THE FOUNDERS: William Worthington Chipman, left, and Gideon Aughinbaugh purchased the *Bolsa de Encinal* from Don Antonio Peralta. No known photo of Gideon Aughinbaugh exists. He rests in Plot 39 in Oakland's Mountain View Cemetery. Aughinbaugh died in 1897; his grave remained unmarked until the Alameda Historical Society remembered Alameda's co-founder with this red granite marker in 1980.

The Town of Alameda

This map shows Chipman and Aughinbaugh's town about 1878. In an early 1880s interview for Myron. W. Woods' *History of Alameda County,* Aughingbaugh said they hired the "silver-tongued" Colonel (Henry) Fitch to sell the lots, which "fetched an average price of $80 a lot." The map shows property owners to the north and east of town. They include W. N. Hawley, a retired merchant who lived in San Francisco with his wife, Maria, and four daughters. Their household included a domestic servant and an hostler, who took care of the horses. Louisa Haile had come to Alameda with her husband, physician Dr. Henry Haile, from Vermont. They had two children, Carson and Ellen. G.G. Briggs was a fruit dealer from New York who lived in Oakland with his wife, whom the 1870 census lists as "E.G." They had three children: Mary, George and Theodore. Briggs Street, which defined one of their property boundaries, is named for the family. The South Pacific Coast Railroad's Pacific Land Investment Company had purchased the railroad's right-of-way along Monroe Street just south of the Briggs' property.

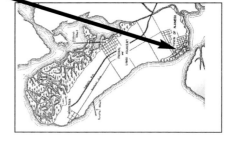

Take a hike!
Stroll around the Town of Alameda

I n 1883, Myron W. Wood published the *History of Alameda County, California*. While writing the book, Wood's historian, J. P. Monro-Fraser, sat down with Alameda co-founder Gideon Aughinbaugh and held what Monro-Fraser called "a lengthy interview."

Aughinbaugh told Monro-Fraser that rather than pursuing his trade as a carpenter, he decided to go into the more lucrative grocery business. He and his wife, Edith, opened a store near today's First and Mission streets in San Francisco.

As they sold foodstuffs to their neighbors, the Aughinbaughs noticed a vein of gold that they hoped

A HIKE THROUGH THE OLD TOWN OF ALAMEDA
will reveal some surprising facts about the Island City's past. The numbers on the map refer to stops along the way.

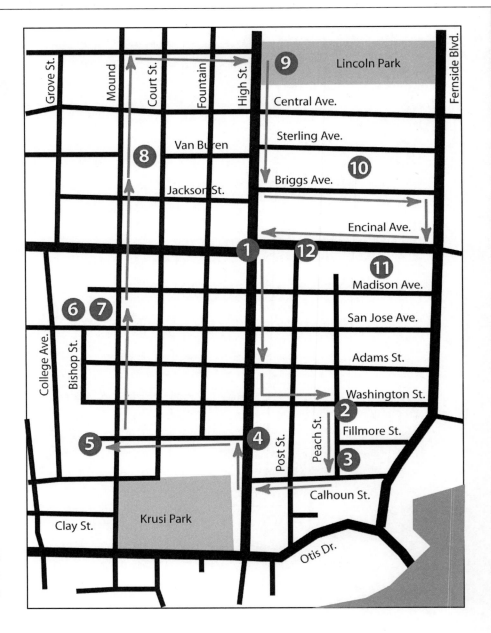

THE BOUNDARIES of the original Town of Alameda are still evident in George Cram's 1908 map. Notice that a waterway is still flowing through the southern end of the town.

to mine. This gold was not in the far-away Sierra Nevada, but right in front of them on their grocery store shelves: fresh fruit. Gideon and Edith were astonished at how much money people were willing to pay for fruit like peaches, apples and cherries. They dreamed of a way to raise their own fruit, but knew they needed land to do this.

Chipman's "intelligence office"

Perhaps Gideon and Edith had visited the reading room and "intelligence office" on Clay Street just a block down from Portsmouth Plaza. They could keep up on news in the east by reading the newspapers that Vermont native William

Worthington Chipman kept there. Historian Imelda Merlin tells us that the Aughinbaughs would have found "newspapers from the chief towns in the United States and a 'Miners' and Strangers' Register'" at Chipman's office. Chipman headed west early in life, first to Ohio where he worked a school principal and studied law. He came to San Francisco in 1850.

Aughinbaugh told Monro-Fraser that he "came over (to the *Bolsa de Encinal*, as the Alameda peninsula was known) in September 1850, with Chipman."

The enterprising pair "subleased from Depachier and Le Maitre 160 acres fronting on San Francisco Bay." (The men Aughinbaugh remembered as Depachier and Le Maitre were Joseph Depassier and Balthazar Maitre who had leased the *Bolsa de Encinal* from Don Antonio Peralta.)

In 1895, two years before his death, Aughinbaugh granted a second interview; this one to the publisher of the *Alameda Daily Argus*. "Aughinbaugh (unlike Chipman) was not in the habit of keeping a diary," writes historian Woody Minor in a 1990 *Alameda Journal* article. Minor writes that not only was the interview published in the May 16, 1895, *Alameda Argus* but a copy of the interview found its way into the City Hall cornerstone that was laid that same day.

Striking gold

In the second interview Aughinbaugh remembers ordering 1,000 fruit trees, which arrived in May 1851 in an express shipment. By July the partners had their first peach; in September they were ready to bring their first fruits to market. They had indeed struck gold; they were able to sell the peaches, some for the princely sum of $1 each. One month later on October 22, 1851, they purchased the peninsula from Don Antonio. Chipman and Aughinbaugh now owned their very own vein of gold not in the far-away Sierra, but nearer the marketplace where they could cash in much more quickly.

In order to raise the money to pay for the peninsula, Chipman and Aughinbaugh sold portions of their land to other enterprising Yankees, but kept the East End for themselves. In 1853, they hired surveyor J F. Stratton to survey the Town of Alameda for them and teamed up with Stratton to lay out streets.

They named the streets running east-west for presidents and other political luminaries of the day: Van Buren, Madison, Jefferson, Clay and Calhoun, for example. They christened the north-south streets to suit the landscape: Mound, Peach, Market and Post to name four. They named the main north-south road "High Street" and planned to connect it to the road running into the hills toward the redwoods.

Let's take a hike

The spot where Monroe and High streets intersect became the town's focal point with a hotel and a tannery (Monroe Street later became Encinal Avenue.) Let's start our hike here and explore the town.

The northwest corner of today's High Street and Encinal Avenue (1) boasts a Queen Anne-style building once home to the Hotel Encinal. Listen carefully and perhaps you'll hear the faint echo of a South Pacific Coast Railroad train pulling into the station just across High Street. These trains

In order to raise the money to pay Don Antonio Peralta for the peninsula, Chipman and Aughinbaugh sold portions of their land to other enterprising Yankees, but kept the East End for themselves.

began running in 1878, long after Chipman and Aughinbaugh laid out their town.

Cross Encinal Avenue, and walk south along High Street to Washington Street. Take a left on Washington and walk one block to Peach Street (2). This is where Chipman and Aughinbaugh built their first house. In her book, *Alameda: A Geographical History*, Imelda Merlin describes the two-story, seven-room dwelling as a "knocked-down house brought around the Horn."

Continue down Peach one block to Fillmore Street (3). Had you stood here in 1853, you would have been standing on the shore of an inlet from San Leandro Bay. The town's wharf once jutted into this inlet here.

When you compare the modern-day map with the 1875 map, you'll notice that the old shoreline interrupted Fillmore Street between Peach (3) and High streets (4). You'll have to "cross the water" down Peach to Calhoun Street, walk left on Calhoun, then right on High Street to

Take a hike! The Town of Alaemda

About the year 1858 there were about a half dozen bodies buried at the intersection of Mound and Jefferson streets in Old Alameda. The last of these graves were taken up a few months ago.

—The Alameda Semi-Weekly Argus

July 13, 1889

reach Fillmore (4) again. Take a left at Fillmore and you'll notice the street ends after just one short block. A glance at the 1875 map will show you why: The end of Fillmore was the end of town.

Return to Mound Street and walk left. Stop at San Jose Avenue. A look at the map of the old town will reveal that San Jose Avenue was once called Jefferson Street and that the intersection of Jefferson and Mound streets skirted the edge of town. Peter Parfait's home (6) and the town's cemetery (7) were located near this intersection.

In her book, Merlin notes an interview with M. W. Peck. Peck was an "old salt" who had been living in Alameda since at least 1860. In 1909 Peck recalled an "adobe pile belonging to a French fisherman Peter Parfe and his Indian wife." Peck's spelling of the fisherman's last name and his notion of the "fisherman's" origin were both incorrect:

Peter Parfait was a Belgian who made his home near the intersection of Jefferson (today's San Jose Avenue) and Mound streets with his Native American wife whose name is lost to us. He arrived at least two years before Chipman and Aughinbaugh set foot on the peninsula.

Merlin says that Parfait died in 1865, He was buried somewhere on the peninsula. The fate of his wife is lost to us. Merlin tells us that she simply disappeared.

The town's cemetery

I would like to speculate that Parfait was laid to rest near his home. I say this because near this very spot stood Alameda's first (and—as far as we know—only) cemetery. While researching this hike I came across an article that historian Woody Minor had written for the *Alameda Journal* in 1990. In it Minor presented a story that appeared in the July 13, 1889, issue of the *Alameda Semi-Weekly Argus*. The article describes a small cemetery located here.

"I remember that about the year 1858 there were about a half dozen bodies buried at the intersection of Mound and Jefferson streets in Old Alameda," the *Argus* said. "At that time the town lay wholly east of High Street. By coming west on Jefferson Street several blocks they no doubt thought they were getting beyond the settlement. The last of these graves were taken up a few months ago."

It remains unclear just where the remains of these half dozen souls ended up; perhaps they now rest at Mountain View Cemetery in Oakland.

Dreams of a county seat

Continue walking north on Mound Street to Santa Clara Avenue. As you walk the four blocks between Encinal and Santa Clara avenues, realize you are in the part of town that Chipman and Aughinbaugh had reserved for something very special. They hoped to convince the Alameda County nabobs to locate the county seat here. This explains the name of the streets "Court" and "Fountain" as two of the several landmarks the founders envisioned for this part of town. When you reach Van Buren Avenue and Court Street (G), stop and have a look at the earlier maps. You'll notice that that Van Buren was not always interrupted here and once continued right through this housing development.

Cyrus Wilson School

The area bounded by Van Buren and Jackson avenues and Court and Mound streets was once home to the Cyrus Wilson School (8). The 1875 map designates this property as Block 92. We know from M. W. Wood's *History of Alameda County* that "Rev. A. M. Myers offered to sell to the (school) trustees two lots in Block 92 for $60." The trustees took Myers up on his offer, bought the property and erected a school on the site. This school replaced the town's first school house, a one-room cabin, which stood at the edge of town on Jefferson Street.

Cyrus Wilson served as one of the town's early trustees. The school bore his name until 1909, the 100th anniversary of Abraham Lincoln's birth. Alameda got a heavy dose of the "Lincoln-mania" that was sweeping over the land.

"Across the nation people hastened to devise, construct, adapt, and re-christen various memorials in his honor," writes historian Judith Lynch.

Wilson's legacy was lost and his eponymous school was renamed Lincoln School. Alamedans didn't stop there, however: at the same time they renamed Railroad Avenue for the 16th president and christened Lincoln Park, our next stop on the hike.

BUILT IN 1893 the Cyrus Wilson School once stood on Van Buren Street on the peninsula's East End.

Continue walking north on Mound Street until you reach Santa Clara Avenue. Stop for a moment; you are standing very near the Sather Mound, which stood here from pre-historic times until its final destruction in 1908. Walk west along Santa Clara to High Street and Lincoln Park.

The water supply

As you enter the park (9) you'll walk past some ornate "street furniture": the wrought-iron fence and gate to Robert R. Thompson's estate. Thompson was the brains (and brawn) behind the Artesian Water Works. He built a home here in 1881, which fire destroyed just four years later; all we have to remind us of the Thompson estate is the cast-iron fence. (While you're here have a look at the plaque commemorating the Sather Mound. You'll see it about 25 yards just past the gate.)

Return to High Street and walk south to Briggs Avenue; walk left on Briggs. As you walk down this street (10) to Fernside Avenue, picture the orchards that once stood here.

(Try to picture what the 1,000 fruit trees that Chipman and Aughinbaugh planted south of here must have looked like—especially when they were in bloom.) The street you're on was named for the property owners here. You can see their name on the 1875 map—G. G. Briggs was a fruit dealer who lived in Oakland.

Once you reach Fernside Avenue, you're on the edge of town, literally. This street nearly defines the old San Leandro Bay shoreline. You can see this clearly if you have a look at the map on page 15.

As you walk down Briggs Street to Fernside Avenue, picture the orchards that once stood here. (And try to picture what the 1,000 fruit trees Chipman and Aughinbaugh planted south of here must have looked like—especially when they were in bloom.)

Walk right on Fernside until you reach Madison Street. Take a right on Madison. Stop for a moment and have a look at all that's left of Market Street (11).

When you compare the map on page 15 with the one on page 17 you'll see that Market Street once ran the length of the town; now it's just a stump of its old self. Continue down Madison until you reach Post Street; take a right to return to Encinal Avenue. The fountain (12) on Encinal stands at the spot of the South Pacific Coast Railroad's High Street Station. Walk just one short block and you will have come full circle.

A LIGHT MAST at Paru Street and San Antonio Avenue, far left, marks the western boundary of the "Town of Encinal and Lands Adjacent." A second light mast, far right, at Park Street and Encinal Avenue marks the eastern boundary. "San Antonio Creek" (today's estuary) and San Francisco Bay defined the property's north-south boundaries.

Take a hike! The Town of Encinal

'Lands Adjacent to the Town of Encinal'

The western boundary of "Hibbard's Third's" was Paru Street; the eastern boundary morphed into Park Street.

The dotted line on the map outlines the Town of Encinal.

Hibbard named east-west streets north of Central Avenue for birds; all but Eagle have been renamed.

He named the north-south streets for fish. All but Paru have been renamed. Leviathan Street led to Hibbard's Wharf.

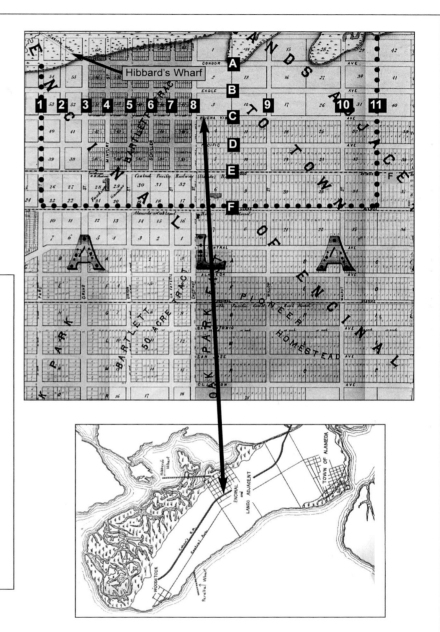

The "bird-street" changes from north to south (corresponding letters are on the 1875 map, right). All are "avenues":

A. Condor> Clement

B. Eagle *Street* became Eagle *Avenue*

C. Falcon > Buena Vista

D. Dove > Pacific

E. Linnet > Railroad (later Lincoln)

F. Quail > Santa Clara

The "fish-street"changes from west to east (corresponding numbers are on the 1875 map, right). All are "streets":

1. Paru did not change
2. Perch > Hibbard
3. Leviathan > Grand
4. Dolphin >Minturn
5. Pike > Union
6. Trout, > Schiller
7. Salmon > Lafayette
8. Minnow > Chestnut
9. Bass > Willow
10. Pampino > Walnut
11. Mullett > Oak

Take a hike!

Stroll around 'Hibbard's Third'

In 1851 when wages hovered around $1 a day, it would have taken almost 45 years for the average worker in the United States working six days a week to earn the $14,000 that Chipman and Aughingbaugh paid for their peninsula. At the time, gold was trading at $15 an ounce, so $14,000 equaled 933 ounces of gold.

In order to raise this kind of money, the new owners would have to sell about 56,000 pieces of fruit at 25 cents each in a year's time: that comes to 56 peaches or apples from each of the 1,000 trees they had planted. They knew the trees could yield a good crop, but could not

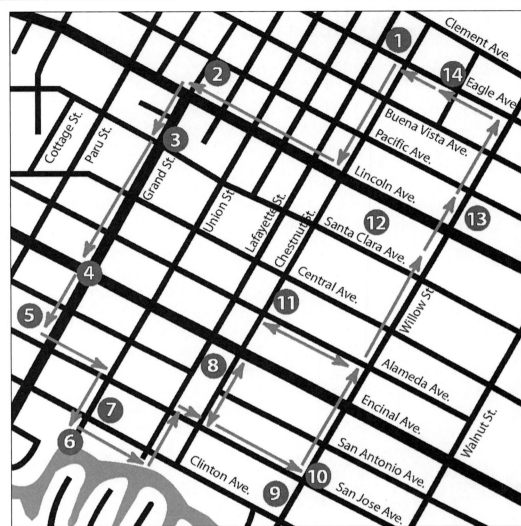

EARLY MAPS LABELED HIBBARD'S THIRD as "Lands Adjacent to the Town of Encinal." The town itself is outlined on the map on page 23. This hike will take you through the entire "Hibbard's Third" and show you its various layers of development.

chance bringing in so rich a harvest in their first season. They did have an alternative. The pair could turn to other land-hungry newcomers and sell parts of the peninsula to them, and that's what they decided to do. One of these was James Hibbard, a man the 1852 California census listed as 35-year-old physician "J. F. Hebbrid."

Failed to pay

The census taker noted that "Dr. Hebbrid" was originally from Ohio and had made his way to California by way of Maryland. Hibbard promised to pay Chipman and Aughinbaugh $4,666.66 for 656.6 acres. The property first became knows as "Hibbard's Third" and later "Lands Adjacent to the Town of Encinal."

Court records reveal that the good doctor reneged and failed to pay for his property. Despite not ponying up, Hibbard laid out a town he dubbed "Encinal."

A look at the map of "Lands Adjacent to the Town of Encinal" shows Hibbard's streets; just two—Eagle and Paru—still have their original names. However, in keeping with city ordinances, all east-west thoroughfares became "avenues"; Eagle Street became Eagle Avenue.

Let's start our walk at Eagle Avenue and Chestnut Street (1). Had you been on this spot prior to 1872 you would have been at the intersection of Eagle and Minnow streets. Walk south on Chestnut Street to Lincoln Avenue.

Chestnut Street has the distinction of being one of the first streets on the peninsula to be paved and lined

Chestnut Street has the distinction of being one of the first streets to be paved and lined with sidewalks; this in a day when the good citizens found it necessary to employ someone to "water" the streets to keep the dust down.

with sidewalks; this in a day when the good citizens found it necessary to employ someone to "water" the streets to keep the dust down. Imelda Merlin tells us that the city's first "street-sprinkling system" comprised "a cart drawn by four horses (that) wetted down the main streets of Alameda."

Paving the way

In 1874, Columbus Bartlett paved Chestnut Street and laid out sidewalks along each side. Bartlett no doubt took his inspiration from nearby Pacific Avenue (the former Dove Street), which the Oakland Paving Company had "modernized" one year earlier.

Walk up to Lincoln Avenue and go right to Grand Street (2). In this part of town, Lincoln Avenue first bore the name of a bird, the linnet. When A.A. Cohen's San Francisco and Alameda Railroad began running on tracks

Louis Fassking owned the town's largest hotel and dance pavilion. He hosted moonlight socials and performances by such traveling artists as Tom Thumb.

—**Woody Minor**

WHAT'S LEFT: This home on Eagle Avenue carries a secret. It's the remnants of Fassking's Park & Hotel that once anchored the intersection of Dolphin and Linnett streets (today's Grand Street and Lincoln Avenue).

laid on Linnet Street, the name was changed to Railroad Avenue, then later to Lincoln.

All aboard for Fassking's!

The SF&A train station, which Cohen dubbed "Encinal" was known colloquially as "Fassking's Railroad Station"; you can see this on the 1875 map. In 1881, the name of the station was changed to Grand Street Station.

Louis Fassking owned what Woody Minor calls "the town's largest hotel (and) dance pavilion here." In *Taking Care of Business*, Minor writes that Fassking hosted "moonlight socials and performances by such traveling artists as Tom Thumb."

Fassking's was bounded by Leviathan (Grand), Linnet (Railroad/Lincoln Avenue), Pike (Union) and Quail (Santa Clara Avenue).The entrance to Fassking's Park & Hotel was at the intersection of Dolphin (Minturn) Street and Linnet (Lincoln Avenue). Today's Minturn Court (3) is on the hotel site; Felix Marcuse and Julius Remmel built

A STRING OF PEARLS: This trio of homes on Grand Street helps define Alameda's Gold Coast. From left to right: The firm of Brehaut and Cornelius built the Charles Shaner-designed home at 1001 Grand Street; Brehaut and Cornelius also built the home at 1007 Grand Street; A. W. Pattiani designed and built the home at 1011 Grand Street.

all the homes in this court after the hotel closed. At about the same time (around 1891) a pair of the hotel's buildings were moved to 2031 and 2033 Eagle Avenue. We'll have a look at them on the last stop on our hike (14).

Walk up Grand Street to Santa Clara Avenue. The Alameda, Oakland and Piedmont Railroad began running horse cars on Santa Clara Avenue from Webster Street to Grand Street in 1875. Minor writes that the AO&P car barns occupied a corner of Fassking's property here. In 1877 the AO&P extended the line to Park Street.

The line was electrified in 1893 and extended across the Park Street Bridge the following year. The AO&P ran horse cars on Santa Clara Avenue from Webster Street to Grand Street. Minor writes that Fassking served the AO&P as a founding director and that the line's car barns occupied a corner of his property at Santa Clara Avenue and Grand Street.

Another rail line, James "Slippery Jim" Fair and Alfred "Hog" Davis's South Pacific Coast Railroad began running in 1878 along today's Encinal Avenue. The nearest stations from our standpoint were: Bay Station at Minnow (Chestnut) to the east (on your left as you face San Francisco Bay) and Morton Street to the west (on your right as you face the bay).

Once you've crossed Encinal Avenue, you're in the Gold Coast, so called from the ritzy homes the wealthy built for themselves along the nearby Bay Shore.

A 'String of Pearls'

One of my favorite sights here is the "String of Pearls" on Grand Street between San Antonio and San Jose avenues. That's the name that Alameda Museum curator George Gunn gave the trio of homes at 1001, 1007 and 1011 Grand.

Take a short walk to the foot of Union Street (6) and have a look at Joseph A. Leonard's brown shingle home, which stood on the Bay Shore until the 1950s, when the Utah Construction Company created South Shore and a place to build those more modern homes you see across the lagoons.

In his book about Leonardville, Minor writes that Leonard—whose company was in the midst of developing the surrounding area—turned to his head draftsman, C. H. Russell, to design his own home.

Joseph A. Leonard's brown shingle home stood on the Bay Shore at the foot of Union Street until the 1950s, when the Utah Construction Company created South Shore and a place to build those more modern homes you see across the lagoons.

Return to Clinton Avenue. Don't miss the "Garratt Mansion" at 900 Union Street (7). Architect Fuller Claflin designed this stately Alameda home in the Colonial Revival style for brass foundry scion W. T. Garratt, Jr. Now walk right one block to Lafayette Street. Take a short detour left to see St. Joseph Basilica (8).

Return to San Jose Avenue and walk to Willow Street. Stop at the striking home at 2070 San Jose Avenue (9). Architect David Brehaut built it as a "salesman sample" to impress prospective clients.

Walk left down Willow Street. Stop and have a look at 1016 Willow Street (10). This Queen Anne-style cottage was built in 1877 for Henry B. Mullen and is one of oldest houses on the street.

When you reach Alameda Avenue, walk left to see the Meyers House and Gardens at 2021 Alameda Avenue. (11)

Take a hike! The Town of Encinal

Return to Willow Street and walk left. Stop and have a look at the Stick-style cottage at 1527 Willow (12). We have a vintage photograph of this home. George Gunn tells us that it came it from a "glass negative found in the loft of a garage."

Denis Straub built the home at 1610 Willow Street (13); his stepson Fred Philip Fischer designed the home. Straub married Fred's mother and taught the Fischer boys the building trade. Fred Philip also designed the home on this book's cover.

An echo of the past

The last stop on the tour (14) truly echoes Alameda's past. The homes at 2031 and 2033 Eagle Avenue once stood on Lincoln Avenue between Grand and Union streets (3) as part of Louis Fassking's Park & Hotel. Gunn says it was built before 1872 and moved to this location in 1891.

The streetcars and most of the street names are gone; it seems this remnant of Fassking's Park & Hotel is all there to remind us of what was once the Town of Encinal.

ALL IN THE FAMILY: Fred Philip Fischer designed this Willow Street home; his stepfather Denis Straub built it. The home's fish-scale shingles and rows of spindles set it apart as a fine example of a Queen Anne-style house. The balcony makes the home particularly attractive.

WAITING FOR THE TRAIN? Women and children mingle with a work crew in front of the car barn that A.A. Cohen built for the San Francisco & Alameda Railroad; a locomotive peeks out behind them. The tracks in the right center of the photograph led out to "Cohen's Wharf" on San Francisco Bay. This photograph came from the Lawrence & Houseworth collection. George Lawrence and Thomas Houseworth opened the first optical shop in San Francisco. In 1859, they began taking photographs and sold them out of their business on Montgomery Street, inset. They turned many of their photographs into stereoscopic pairs. Did you notice the young man running into main the photograph on the far left?

Take a hike! The Town of Woodstock

Take a hike!

The Town of Woodstock

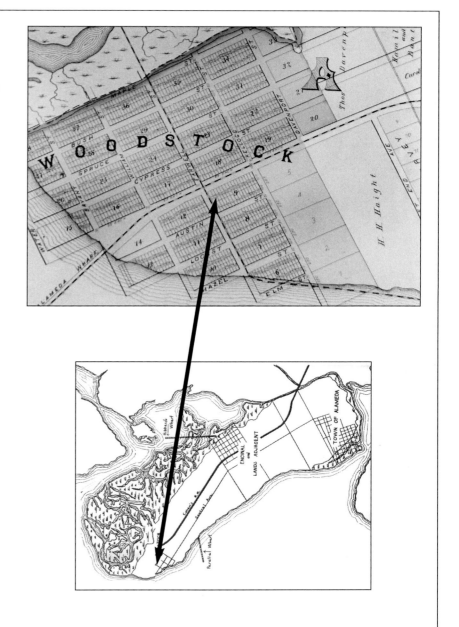

While many Alamedans associate Woodstock with the Alameda Housing Authority's 1941 housing project, the area has a much deeper and richer history that stretches back 90 years before the project appeared. In 1851 or early 1852 Charles Bowman received a deed from Chipman and Aughinbaugh for land here. And the Town of Woodstock was the 1864 creation of A.A. Cohen and his partner J. D. Farwell.

Let's take a hike and uncover some of this history. By the time we're finished we will have met a young Jack London, learned about the terra cotta, borax and oil industries and stood on the old bay shore about where A.A. Cohen's San Francisco & Alameda Railroad wharf once stood. We'll also meet an early California governor and see a fine example of a Gothic Revival farmhouse.

Let's get started.

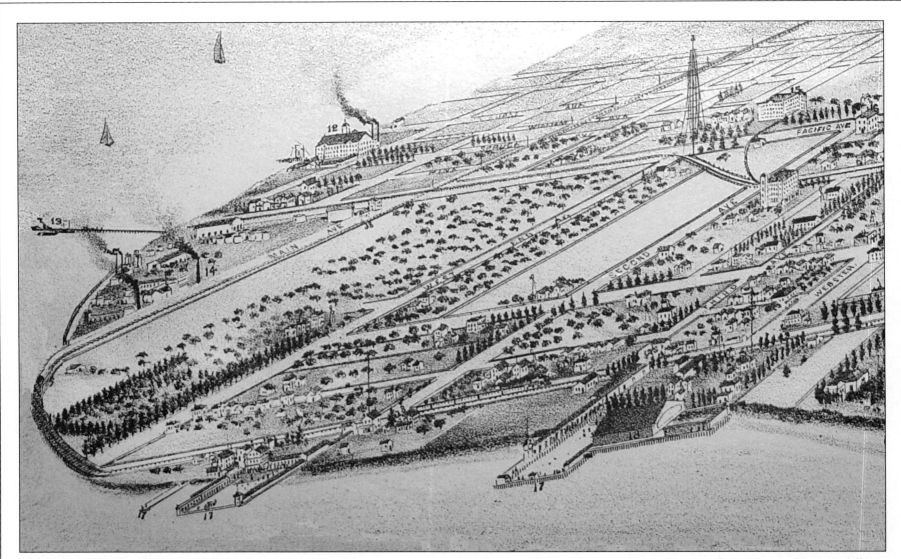

THE BUCOLIC WEST END is shown on the *Alameda Argus* 1888 map. Resorts lay along the southern bay shore, while smoke billows from the more industrial western shore. Included on this map are the home of Gov. Henry H. Haight, the Kohlmoos Hotel, the N. Clark Pottery Works and West End Primary school where writer Jack London attended first grade.

We'll get underway at Lincoln Avenue and Linden Street (1). Longfellow School stands on one side of Lincoln here and Longfellow Park on the other. First the San Francisco & Alameda Railroad, and then Central Pacific Railroad trains ran on tracks on Lincoln here. Longfellow Park was once home to the Kohlmoos Hotel. It's hard to imagine a building the size of the Kohlmoos nestled in a park the size of Longfellow, but such a building stood here until 1934.

In his book about Alameda parks, *Alameda At Play*, Woody Minor says that "the four-story structure (included) self-contained systems for water and gas." The parcel the hotel stood on was bigger than today's park; as Haight Avenue did not appear on maps until 1896. Minor describes the hotel's landscaped grounds as "covering about an acre" and "laid out with paths, fountains and a pavilion for billiards and bowling." Longfellow School just across the street replaced West End Primary School, where 6-year-old Jack London attended classes.

Walk west on Lincoln to Marshall Way and down Marshall Way to Pacific Avenue (2). Marshall Way was built on the San Francisco & Alameda Railroad's right-of-way. A.A. Cohen laid tracks across Alameda on today's Lincoln Avenue in 1864. Cohen's SF&A station and wharf stood at the foot of Pacific Avenue, however. He had to build his

THIS HIKE through Alameda's West End reveals secrets buried beneath layers of history.

tracks in a northwesterly direction somewhere along the line so his trains reached Pacific Avenue and the rail yards. Cohen chose the spot where Marshall Way now runs to build the curve that accomplished this.

Cohen was by no means the first to develop the area. Sometime in late 1851 or early 1852, Charles Bowman purchased 144 acres here from Chipman and Aughinbaugh. Instead of a fence, Bowman chose to build a ditch to define his eastern property boundary. Quickly dubbed "Bowman's Ditch," it ran in a north-south direction from the marshlands to San Francisco Bay. The ditch crossed this area about where Marshall Way and Pacific Avenue intersect.

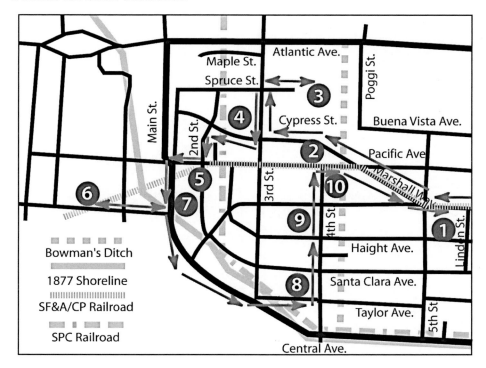

JOHN AND HERMAN KOHLMOOS did a brisk hotel business in this four-story Italianate-style building from 1879 to 1886. The impressive structure stood at the site of today's Longfellow Park until 1934.

Did you know?
George Bird's hometown of Woodstock, England, is also home to Blenheim Castle, Winston Churchill's ancestral home and birthplace.

Nehemiah Clark

Chipman Elementary School—named for one of Alameda's founders—stands where Nehemiah Clark built his terra cotta factory. Before Clark arrived, this piece of land belonged to Thomas Davenport. We'll learn more about him when we reach Woodstock Park. When Davenport died, his heirs sold this portion of his property to Clark.

On his fascinating Web site about California brick making (http://calbricks.netfirms.com), Dan Mosier tells us that Delaware native Nehemiah Clark arrived in California in 1850. In 1864, he established Pacific Pottery on the east side of Sacramento where he made various clay products. These included vitrified sewer pipe, chimney pipe and his best-seller, the "Pacific Fire Brick."

Mosier says that Nehemiah opened an office and depot on Market Street in San Francisco in 1880, where he sold fire brick and other clay products. In 1883, he moved his office to California Street. When he decided to move his pottery plant from Sacramento to be closer to the bustling San Francisco market, he selected a site in Alameda for his new works.

Clark's new plant—an enormous four-story structure built with more than 600,000 of Nehemiah's own bricks—arose at 401 Pacific Avenue. Merlin writes that the Clark factory contained four kilns and at 28,500 square feet was the largest building in Alameda. The building stood until 1963.

Woodstock Park (3) lies behind Chipman School. To get there, walk down Pacific to Third Street; go right on Third Street and right on Spruce Street to the gate at the end of the street. Go through the gate and into the park.

Thomas Davenport

Like the site where Chipman Middle School stands, this land belonged to Thomas Davenport. In fact, Third Street was called Davenport Street on some early maps. Davenport lived on the Woodstock Park site in one of the two mansions in the area. (Governor Henry H. Haight lived in the other.)

The 1880 census lists Thomas living here with his wife, Caroline, his brother Matthew and his cousin James. According to Minor, Thomas made his living as a fur trader in Missouri and a wholesaler in Mexico. He arrived in California during the Gold Rush. Thomas owned 15 acres here and "built his house on the west half of his property, leasing out the remaining land for cultivation," Minor writes.

Farmer John London, his wife, Flora; daughters Eliza and Ida and 4-year-old son, Jack, appear as

ABOVE : CIVIL WAR VETERAN John London, left, married Flora Wellman, right, in 1876. The couple lived in Alameda for almost three years. John raised Flora's son as his own. The young man—Jack London—grew up to be one of America's greatest authors.

BELOW : WHILE IN ALAMEDA Jack attended West End Primary School. The arrow points to the school on the *Alameda Semi-Weekly Argus* 1888 map. See a broader view on page 33.

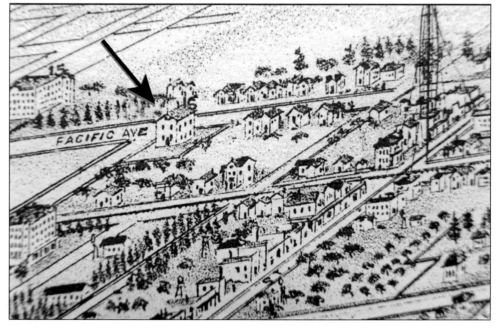

the very next household on the same page of the 1880 federal census as Thomas Davenport.

According to Russ Kingman in *A Pictorial Life of Jack London*, Jack London was born on January 12, 1876, to Flora Wellman at 615 Third Street in San Francisco. Jack's father, astrologist William Chaney, denied paternity and left town.

About nine months later on September 7, Flora married partially disabled Civil War veteran John London. The following year, John removed Eliza and Ida—daughters from a previous marriage—from the Protestant Orphan Asylum on Haight Street in San Francisco.

On to the East Bay

Sometime in 1878 a diphtheria epidemic swept through San Francisco. Jack and his stepsister Eliza both suffered near-fatal attacks of the disease. Kingman says that the London family moved from San Francisco to Oakland to escape the epidemic; by 1879 John London was operating a truck garden on a parcel of land in Oakland near the present-day Emeryville border.

Then in 1880, when John ("Johnny" to his family) was 4 years old, John Sr. and Flora moved to Alameda with the children. According to Kingman, John and Flora cultivated 20 acres of land near Thomas Davenport's mansion. Two years later, 6-year-old Johnny started grade school at West End Primary School (on the site of today's Longfellow School). The Londons didn't stay long. On January 7, 1883, John pulled up roots and moved his family to the Tobin Ranch in San Mateo

County where they raised horses and grew potatoes. It's likely that the family's departure is tied to Thomas Davenport's death the same year. Davenport owned the property the Londons were farming.

Return to Spruce Street and walk back to Third Street. Walk left on Third and right on Cypress Street.

As you walk along Cypress toward Second Street, you'll find yourself in the heart of modern-day Woodstock. The homes here are part of an Alameda Housing Authority development completed in September 1941.

In a 1991 article he wrote for the *Alameda Journal*, Woody Minor says that the project comprised 22 acres bordered by Pacific Street on the south, Brush Street on the north, Main Street on the west and Third Street on the east.

"Woodstock's careful design, high quality construction and post-war history as a homeowners' cooperative give it a distinguished place in Alameda's recent history," Minor wrote.

Take a left on Second Avenue and stop for a moment.

Bird's Hotel

A little more than 80 years before the Alameda Housing Authority came on the scene, this same plot of ground (just about where you're standing now) was home to Bird's Hotel. We can thank artist Joseph Lee for his 1868 painting, "Bird's Hotel, Bird's Point." A.A. Cohen commissioned Lee to do the painting to celebrate the 1864 completion of his San Francisco & Alameda Railroad. Lee's painting shows "opening day" on the railroad with the locomotive *J.G. Kellogg* pulling its passenger-laden cars onto his wharf. Close inspection of Lee's painting reveals the ferry boat *Sophie McLane* arriving to meet the passengers; even closer inspection (and a little knowledge about the painting's story) reveals even more detail.

The painting includes the SF&A car barn, Bird's Hotel and a surprise—George Bird himself as a hunter in the painting's foreground.

It seems George Bird and A.A. Cohen had more in common than just owning property on Bowman's Point—they both hailed from England—Cohen from London and Bird from Woodstock. So when Cohen laid out the town of which you see vestiges on the 1885 map, he named it for his fellow countryman's hometown, Woodstock.

The SPCRR rolls through town

When the South Pacific Coast Railroad began running in 1878, its track cut a swath right through the property about where Bird's Hotel had stood. Another look at the 1885 map shows "Kellogg Street"—named, perhaps, for Cohen's locomotive. It's likely that the SPCRR used this right-of-way to send its trains barreling towards its pier across the marshlands.

Continue walking down Second Street until you reach Pacific Avenue. Look across Pacific; the entire square here was home to the San Francisco & Alameda Railroad's car barn. We have a wonderful photograph of the car barn. The 1885 map shows where the SF&A tracks "bent" to accommodate the SF&A's car barn.

This is historic ground.

It was here on September 6, 1869, that the first transcontinental railroad train arrived from Sacramento and points east.

This area with its wharf served as the transcontinental railroad's western terminus until November 8, 1869, when the Central Pacific Railroad began running its trains into Oakland instead. Four years later the CPRR sent all its trains to Oakland over the Alice Street Bridge. Trains ran on today's Constitution Way towards the bridge.

The tracks to "Cohen's Wharf" remained open as spur lines to Woodstock's growing industry. Walk down Pacific Avenue and cross Main Street and go about 20 yards past the fence. You're now standing on the old shoreline.

Look out to your left at a 45 degree angle and imagine Cohen's Wharf jutting out into San Francisco Bay

THIS DETAIL from the *Alameda Semi-Weekly Argus* 1888 map shows the Pacific Coast Oil Works, "Cohen's Wharf" and William Tell Coleman's borax works.

here. Cohen had to build the wharf 3,750 feet into the bay in order to reach water deep enough to suit the ferry boats.

The CPRR abandoned this wharf in 1873, but we know from the 1888 *Alameda Argus* map that it did not fall into disuse. By then the E. M Derby Company was using it as a lumber wharf.

Industrial Woodstock

Two thriving business stood on the shoreline here.

In 1879, the Pacific Coast Oil Works built a kerosene refinery just across the railroad tracks to the south. Three years later, William Tell Coleman began refining borax just to the north.

Primarily used as a fuel for lighting sources, kerosene was the first petroleum product refined on a large scale as the demand for this fuel grew with the population. Until Lloyd Tevis appeared on the scene, most of this precious liquid was imported from the East Coast and the Midwest. Tevis, a former president of Wells Fargo Express Co. and William Randolph Hearst's father, George W. Hearst, founder of the Homestake Mining Co., teamed up to form the Pacific Coast Oil Works. Partners in the venture included Charles Felton, who both ran the U.S. mint in San Francisco, and Felton's brother-in-law George Loomis, a dry goods dealer. They formed Pacific Coast Oil on September 10, 1879. (ChevronTexaco, which evolved from Pacific Coast Oil, celebrates September 10 as its birthday.)

"Pacific Coast soon opened its first refinery, a 600-barrel-per-day operation in Alameda," writes David L. Baker in the *San Francisco Chronicle*. According to Baker, Standard Oil Co acquired Pacific Coast Oil in 1900. Two years later, the new owners dismantled the Alameda operations and moved them to its much larger Richmond refinery. Baker says that Standard Oil used some parts of the Alameda refinery to assemble its new one.

Just to the north, across the SF&A tracks William Tell Coleman built a borax refinery. Borax has many commercial uses as a component of detergents, glass pottery and ceramics, a fire retardant, an insecticide and an ingredient in indelible ink.

ONE OF SEVERAL Pacific Coast Oil Works' stacks looms over the company's refinery on Alameda's western shore.

According to Michael Colbruno on his Mountain View Cemetery blog, Francis Marion "Borax" Smith acquired Coleman's Harmony Borax Works in Death Valley in 1890. Smith combined Coleman's works with his own to form the Pacific Coast Borax Company. Three years later, Smith commissioned the first reinforced concrete building in the United States to house his refinery at the same location of Coleman's original works.

Return to Main Street and walk right. (Main changes its name to Central Avenue here.) Walk along Central to Taylor Avenue; then go along Taylor to Fourth Street.

Meet the governor

Walk left on Fourth Street. You're now on the old West End Avenue, which was the eastern border to Henry H. Haight's estate.

Haight served as California's governor from 1867 to 1871. His home stood about where Fourth Street and Buena Vista Avenue intersect. The 1870 federal census shows Henry and his wife, Anne, living here with three children. The household included a domestic servant, a cook, a laundress and a nurse.

Colbruno tells of Haight's accomplishments as the state's 10th governor. "During his term, the

CALIFORNIA GOVERNOR Henry H. Haight lived in this home with his family. Haight was serving as governor when the University of California came into existence in 1868.

transcontinental railroad was completed, Golden Gate Park was designed, and San Jose Teachers College was established," Colbruno writes. He tells us that the Haight administration reduced the state debt and created the State Board of Health.

Haight lost his seat in a run for re-election. After his defeat, he returned to his law practice, and served as a member of the board of trustees of the University of California.

Henry died in 1878; Anne survived until 1890. The family is buried at Mountain View Cemetery in Oakland.

Continue walking north on Fourth Avenue. Just before you reach Pacific Avenue, you'll see a trim, white Gothic Revival house on your right. This was home to Abram Rich and his family. Read more about this house on pages 45 and 46.

Take a right on Marshall Way and return to the starting point at Lincoln Avenue and Linden Street.

TUDOR REVIVAL: The half-timbering on Dr. William Lum's Gold Coast home leaves no mistake that the architects looked to 16th-century England for inspiration. This home has non-structural elements of a post-and-girt frame.

  A matter of style

Part Two

A matter of style

Our homes reflect the attitude and feelings prevalent at the time they were built. The Greek Revival style recalls that time when—reeling from the British invasion during the War of 1812—America turned with admiration to a contemporary revolution taking place in the very cradle of democracy.

The rustic Gothic Revival style and its urban counterpart, the Italianate style, stem from the fertile minds of Andrew Jackson Downing and Alexander Jackson Davis. These two men did more than any others of their time to express and then shape mid-19th century taste.

The simpler Stick Style reflects the Machine Age and the invention of new tools—especially the scroll saw—and development of the balloon frame.

The exuberant Queen Anne style celebrates the spirit of a time that Samuel Clemens called the "Gilded Age." At the same time (and in the very same place—the 1876 Centennial Exposition in Philadelphia) that Richard Norman Shaw introduced the Queen Anne style, a cleaner, simpler style made

its debut. The Colonial Revival style not only celebrated our country's roots, but gave architects an alternative to Queen Anne's gaudiness. The Shingle style did much the same, erasing gingerbread and replacing it with uncomplicated shingles.

As the 19th century came to an end, history stepped in and played a role forcing architects and builders to go from the elaborate to the simple. Just eight years before Queen Victoria's death brought an end to the era that bore her name, a run on the gold supply precipitated the Panic of 1893—the worst economic crisis to hit the United States to that point in its history.

Customers invaded their banks attempting to redeem silver notes for gold. When the gold supply reached its statutory limit for the minimum amount in federal reserves, people could no longer redeem paper money. Some 500 banks closed their doors; deposits (and life savings) evaporated.

Major railroads failed—among them the Northern Pacific Railway, the Union Pacific and the Atchison, Topeka & Santa Fe. More than 15,000 companies went bankrupt, including Alameda's Joseph Leonard and Company, which closed its doors in 1898.

Small companies, like Leonard's, and their workers bore the brunt. In 1890 unemployment stood at an acceptable 4 percent; three years later it stood at 11.7 percent. It peaked at 18.4 percent the year after the Panic. It fell to 13.7 percent in 1895 but remained in double digits through 1898. The economy finally recovered in 1900. Everyone took a breath, but six years later the Great San Francisco Earthquake and Fire struck, followed closely by the Panic of 1907.

In the meantime, artisans stepped in and brought us the Craftsman style with its simple, straightforward approach; things got even simpler with the coming of the bungalow.

Before we embark on our journey to have a look at these styles in turn, let's get better acquainted with Downing and Davis, the men whose ideas inspired a generation.

THE APOSTLE OF TASTE: Andrew Jackson Downing was one of our country's most important pre-Civil War designers and writers. He began his career as a landscaper and founded the magazine, *The Horticulturist.*

NOTED ARCHITECT Alexander Jackson Davis gained fame and recognition for his "picturesque cottages and villas," in the Gothic Revival and Italianate styles.

Meet the AJDs

An apostle and an architect

A love of the landscape flowed through Andrew Jackson Downing's veins. His father was a wheelwright and a gardener; young Andrew worked in the family nursery. The written word shaped Alexander Jackson Davis's early life. His father was a bookseller and editor. The pair worked together to help shape 19th-century attitudes about architecture and landscape gardening.

In 1841 Downing wrote *A Treatise on the Theory and Practice of Landscape Gardening.* Instead of using Europe as an example, Downing adapted his book to North America,

the first time anyone had done this, and it was eagerly received. The book caught Davis's eye and the following year, the pair collaborated on the tome *Cottage Residences.* Their popular and influential collaboration contributed to the spread of the Carpenter Gothic and Bracketed Italianate architectural styles.

By the time they met, each had established himself in his own profession: Downing as an author and landscape designer and Davis as a lithographer and architect.

In 1826, Davis began working for Ithiel Town and Martin E. Thompson, the most prestigious architectural firm of the Greek Revival. In Washington, Davis designed the Executive Department offices and the first Patent Office building in Washington, D.C.

Davis also designed the Custom House in New York City. In 1831 he was elected an associate member of the

National Academy of Design. In 1835, Davis began working on his book *Rural Residences*, the first pattern book for Gothic Revival homes. Two years later, he helped found the American Institute of Architects in 1837. Davis continued his partnership with Town until shortly before Town's death in 1844.

By the mid-1840s Downing had firmly established a reputation that made him a celebrity of his day. While in London in 1850, a collection of landscape watercolors that Calvert Vaux had painted caught his eye .

Vaux impressed Davis so much that he persuaded the artist to come to the United States and work with him. In 1851 they worked on the U.S. Capitol and the White House grounds and on estates in New York.

Downing met a tragic end on July 28, 1852, while on a boat ride on the Hudson River. The boat caught fire from engines overheated by its negligent captain, who was attempting to outrace another boat to New York City. As people jumped overboard, Downing threw chairs to them as life preservers, and he was evidently swallowed by the river as he tried to save those unable to swim. A few ashen remains and his clothes were rescued days later. His family interred these few remains in Cedar Hill Cemetery, in Newburgh, New York. Vaux took over Downing's architectural practice. He later formed a partnership with Frederick Law Olmsted, with whom he designed Central Park..

BY THE BOOK: This rustic example of a Gothic Revival cottage from A.J. Davis and A.J Downing's book *Rural Cottages* portrays the authors' ideal harmony between nature and architecture.

Did you know?
Carpenter Gothic refers to small buildings in the Gothic Revival style whose designs were simple enough to be executed by a carpenter rather than an architect. Alameda has two fine examples of Carpenter Gothic; in the Webster House and the Rich family home.

In the late 1850s, Davis worked with the entrepreneur Llewellyn S. Haskell to create Llewellyn Park in West Orange, New Jersey, a garden suburb and one of the first planned residential communities in the United States. He died there in 1892 at the age of 90. He rests in Bloomfield Cemetery in Bloomfield, New Jersey.

Both Downing and Davis played major roles in shaping mid-19th century tastes. They deserve special mention in any story that touches on Victorian-era architecture and landscape.

BRRRR! "Icicles" drip from the bargeboards on the Webster House on Versailles Avenue. The bargeboards and the front-facing gable with its smaller counterparts on the roof are components of the Gothic Revival Style.

Gothic Revival

NO ICICLES drip from the plain bargeboards on this Gothic Revival home on Fourth Street, which boasts a simpler design than the Webster House.

By 1878, four Alameda families were living in homes built in a style that was already more than 100 years old when Queen Victoria took the throne in 1837. The Gothic Revival style began in England in 1733 when Henry Pelham built Esher Place in Surrey. Alexander Jackson Davis introduced the style to America in 1838 with his creation "Lyndhurst" in Tarrytown, New York.

Some think that Pelham and Davis were drawing on a style that had never died, so no "revival" was necessary. During a visit to England, I toured York Minster, the largest Gothic-style church north of the Alps. There a stonemason spoke to us on a tour through the Minster.

"Construction on the present church began in 1220 and has never ceased," said the stonemason. "So how can we speak of a revival?" He pointed with his cone-shaped mallet to the 21st-century corbel he was shaping.

Taking the stonemason's enthusiastic and pointed argument at face value, one can still speak of a revival, however. According to Megan Aldrich in *Gothic Revival,* the word Gothic did not describe any style until the 17th century. Then, scholars—looking to the Renaissance as the apex of thought—applied the term to a style they saw as rooted in the "Dark Ages."

Renaissance scholars associated the Goths and their invasion of Europe as the beginning of these shadowy times and applied the term "Gothic" as a pejorative.

Aldrich points to Sir Henry Wooton's description of the Gothic arch as one of "natural imbecility." Sir Christopher Wren, who designed London's St. Paul's Cathedral in the neo-Classical style, saw Gothic architecture as "full of fret and lamentable images."

American Gothic

Andrew Jackson Downing promoted the Gothic Revival style in America in his 1842 book *Cottage Residences,* which mixed romantic architecture with the pastoral picturesque architecture of the

"ROSE COTTAGE": Sea captain Ned Wakeman lived in this Gothic Revival-style home with his wife, Mary, in Oakland. The home once stood near the estuary on Oakland's 10th Avenue.

English countryside with its cottages—simple dwellings void of the exotic trappings that Downing feared were not good for the soul. By the time Downing published his second book, *The Architecture of Country Houses*, in 1850, a pair of innovations allowed builders to construct homes on a larger scale: balloon framing and the jig saw. These advancements, along with the proliferation of pattern books, allowed builders to construct Gothic Revival homes on a much larger scale.

Alameda Gothic

One of Alameda's Gothic Revival gems, the Webster House, began life in New York as an A. J. Downing-designed home. John Nelson Webster had the home milled in New York and shipped around Cape Horn in the hull of the bark *Henry Harbeck*.

In March 1849, Webster joined the Mohawk Mining Company and sailed to California. Each member of 28-man company put in $100 worth of goods as his share. The *Henry Harbeck* sailed around Cape Horn and arrived in San Francisco after a 193-day voyage on September 17, 1849. It took the Mohawk Mining Company until about December 1 to sell its goods. It no doubt delighted the company's members to learn their $100 shares had increased in value to $500. Each member took his profit and struck out on his own.

In December 1850 Webster returned to New York for a visit. While there, he married Caroline Washburn. The couple returned to California on the same ship that had taken John Nelson Webster to California in 1849. This time John Nelson and Caroline had their new home tucked in the *Henry Harbeck's* hold. Gothic Revival style arrived in Alameda in 1854 when John had his ready-made home assembled on what was then Madison Street. Three more homes in this earliest of styles would appear on the scene. On May 20, 1865, Abram and Caroline Rich moved into their Gothic Revival home on what would become Fourth Street.

At about the same time William Jaquith built a Gothic Revival home on Walnut Street at Buena Vista Avenue. And by 1872 the Witgen family was living in their Gothic Revival home along the tracks on Railroad Avenue (Lincoln). In 1902, the Jaquith home was moved up Walnut Street near Railroad Avenue (Lincoln).

Before we look at the Italianate style, let's take a field trip to The J. Mora Moss House in Oakland, visit a Sonoma County home with its wonderful Gothic Revival details and learn about balloon framing.

Field trip!

Oakland's Gothic Revival jewel

The J. Mora Moss House
3612 Webster Street
Oakland, CA 94601

(510) 597-5038

THE J. MORA MOSS HOUSE is a Gothic style Victorian-era home in Oakland's Mosswood Park. This city landmark was built in 1864. The Historic American Buildings Survey calls the home, "One of the finest, if not the finest, existing examples of Gothic architecture of French and English influence as adapted to wood frame domestic architecture to be found in the East Bay, and possibly in Northern California." It is one of five historic homes owned by the City of Oakland and currently serves as an office and storage space for the Oakland Parks and Recreation Department.

Details, details!

Gothic Revival

HERE'S WHAT TO LOOK FOR:

1. High-peaked gables

2. Dormers

3. Finials atop the gables and pendants below them

4. Lacy trim on the eaves and bargeboards (or vergeboards) on the edges of the gables

5. Wide, roofed entry porches

Field trip

Lachryma Montis
at the corner of
West Spain Street and
Third Street West
Sonoma, CA 95476

(707) 938-9559

There is an admission fee.

MARIANO VALLEJO built this Gothic Revival jewel on a 500-acre tract near Sonoma In 1850. The land included a free-flowing spring the Native Americans called *Chiucuyem* (Tears of the Mountain). Vallejo used this name for his new estate, christening it *Lachryma Montis.*

THERE WERE NO RULE BOOKS. Not all Gothic Revival houses have all the elements noted here, for example the Rich home on page 42 has no lacy trim on its bargeboards. Oakland's J. Mora Moss home in Oakland is the best place to see a local Gothic Revival house with many of these details (or you could visit Mariano and Benicia Vallejo's home in Sonoma, above). Compare the Webster House on page 44 to the Moss home on page 47 and you can clearly see the differences between a Carpenter Gothic home and a custom-designed home.

Victorian-era innovation

The frame makes the house

When we stop to admire a Victorian-era home, we often speak of the home's dressing—its style. We think little, however, about the substance that holds it all together—its structure. Style includes the shape and detailing that make up a home's features, both interior and exterior. The features of an Italianate-style home are sharply different than those of a Colonial Revival-style home. All homes, however, regardless of their styles, have two basic structural elements in common: walls and a roof. These require a frame.

During the Victorian era this element evolved from the post-and-girt frame to the braced frame and finally to the balloon frame. Early settlers brought the cumbersome post-and-girt (or timber) frame with them from Europe. Carpenters fashioned mortise-and-tenon joints to connect heavy vertical posts to equally unwieldy horizontal girts, which they held fast with wooden pins or dowels.

Scribe-rule vs. square-rule carpentry

Carpenters employed two different layout methods called scribe-rule carpentry and square-rule carpentry. Scribe-rule carpentry dates from the 12th century. European carpenters brought this method to North America and used it to build structures here from the late 17th into the mid 19th century. Woodworkers using this method had to fashion each and every connection separately, not one interchangeable with the other.

BRACED VS. BALLOON: Thicker posts (D) and braces (E) set the braced frame, right, apart from a later innovation, the lighter balloon frame pictured on page 51.

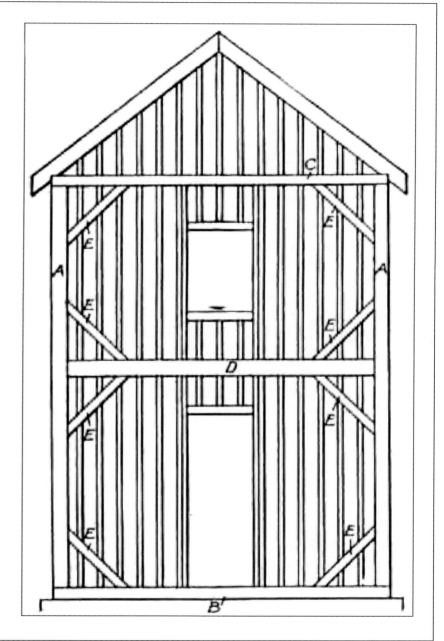

The frame the braces and girts created were visible both inside and outside the home. Wattle-and-daub, brick or rubble with plastered facing filled the spaces between the timbers, creating what was later called the half-timbered style.

Then in the 19th century American carpenters came up with an idea that allowed for interchangable braces and girts and made framing easier: square rule carpentry.

This new type of carpentry introduced uniformity. Carpenters cut timbers to a uniform standard at each joint. Timbers now became interchangeable and allowed the introduction of the braced frame.

Enter the braced frame

Like its predecessor, the braced frame employed heavy posts and girts, but placed lighter 2x4s in between to help support the home's floors and roof. Carpenters added extra stability to this new framing system with corner braces, which gave the frame its name. Braces added a disadvantage for the builder, however, as they interfered with architectural requirements for open spaces for doors, windows and rooms.

Both post-and-girt and braced-frame homes were costly and time-consuming to build and kept homeownership in the realm of the wealthy.

"Houses were expensive and took months to build," writes Kevin Spencer Brown in *Investors Business Daily*. "Cities packed their poor into tenement housing. In rural areas, people put up with rustic cabins or sod dwellings like those of the American Indians."

Then something happened in Chicago that changed all that. Just exactly who thought of the idea and just what

Houses were expensive and took months to build. Then something happened in Chicago that changed all that.

building was the first to utilize it is a matter of some conjecture. One thing remains indisputable, however; the balloon frame revolutionized homebuilding and opened homeownership to more than just the wealthy. Many credit Augustine Taylor with coming up with the idea.

Chicago's Old St. Mary's Church could not afford an elaborate house of worship. They hired Taylor, whose concept was a straightforward one that simplified the building industry.

"He managed to put up a 36-by-24-foot church for the incredibly low price of $400, using do-it-yourself carpenters," Brown writes.

The balloon frame

Taylor eliminated the old mortised beams and fittings. "He replaced them with light 2x4s and 2x6s set close together," writes John H. Leinhard in *Engines of Our Ingenuity*. "He used studs and cross-members. He held the whole thing together with nails—no joints."

Brown points out that—thanks in part to the cheaper, easier-to-build housing Taylor's design inspired—Chicago's population mushroomed from 150 people in 1833 to nearly 30,000 by 1850. Taylor lived to see it reach 1 million.

Besides the cost savings, Taylor's methods let builders break away from the boxy shapes of timber-frame construction. They got far more creative. Soon even the wealthy embraced balloon framing. This allowed Victorian-era architecture to flower.

"The technique swept America," writes Leinhard. "A great gallery of possibility opened up, and people took advantage of it. They built bay windows, watchtowers and gables. They created homes with steeples, cupolas and porches."

Not everyone was impressed, however. Some carpenters dismissed the idea. According to some accounts, the term "balloon" frame was meant as a mocking nickname because the frames looked as flighty as a balloon. Some said the structures would blow away at the first strong wind, a statement that took on special meaning in the Windy City.

Despite the criticism and derision, Taylor's concept caught on. "Its simple, effective and economical manner of construction has materially aided the rapid settlement of the West," wrote George E. Woodward in his highly respected and much-used book *Woodward's Country Houses.*

Woodward quickly dispelled the critics and pointed out the many advantages that the balloon frame offered. He pointed out that the exclusive use of nails to fasten the timber eliminated the need for time-consuming and costly mortice-and-tenon joints. All the elements are interchangeable, he told his reader. And he said that the balloon frame readily adapts to every style of building; its flexibility allows irregular forms.

Solon Robinson, a well-respected author, agricultural journalist, went even further. "If it had not been for the knowledge of the balloon frame, Chicago and San Francisco would never have arisen as they did from little villages to great cities," he wrote.

Much the same can be said of Alameda.

KEEP IT SIMPLE: Posts and braces became completely unnecessary with the introduction of the balloon frame.

FRANKLIN PANCOAST paid the prodigious sum of $4,000 for his Italianate-style home on Everett Street. Perhaps Enoch Pardee's Oakland home, built in 1868 in the same style, influenced the Alameda squatter.

Italianate

In 1870, when Franklin Pancoast hired builder George Severance to build his home in Alameda, about 400 families lived in the township. According to local historian J. Monro-Fraser, Alameda had made "prodigious strides toward prosperity." Most of the township's residents "owned their own premises," Monro-Fraser informed the readers of M. W. Wood's 1883 *History of Alameda County*.

The Central Pacific Railroad's first transcontinental train had crossed the peninsula less than a year before Pancoast hired Severance. And George Lewis had just announced he had started a stagecoach line from Alameda by way of the towns of San Antonio and Brooklyn (in present-day East Oakland) for the less-daring not willing to take advantage of a new-fangled mode of transportation.

Town fathers were also seriously talking about making Oakland more accessible by way of a bridge at Webster Street. Monro-Fraser called the 1870 alternative of reaching the city across the estuary a "weary, plodding journey to the slimy banks of the San Antonio Creek and across it to Oakland."

Pancoast and Severance chose to build a home in the Italianate style and the Pancoast residence has many of the style's features. These include a low-pitched roof, a balanced, symmetrical rectangular shape—disturbed by an addition of a wing on the south side of the home—and tall windows.

The Italianate style began in England in the 1840s, influenced by the late 18th-century Picturesque Movement. Since the turn of

MINE SUPERVISOR D. L. Munson built this Italianate-style home on Eagle Avenue for his family in 1875. The following year, Munson joined other Alameda nabobs as a founding member of the Alameda Loan and Building Association.

the 18th to the 19th century, homes tended to be formal and classical in style. With the Picturesque Movement, however, builders began to design fanciful recreations of Italian Renaissance villas.

Alexander Jackson Davis introduced Italianate as an alternative to Gothic or Greek Revival styles. When the style moved to the United States, builders and designers reinterpreted it, creating a uniquely American style. *Blandwood*, the governor's mansion in North Carolina, completed in 1846, claims to be the oldest example of Italianate architecture in the United States.

One of the earliest—and more famous—Italianate-style homes is San Jose's Fallon House. When Thomas Fallon built the home in 1855, he deliberately made it higher than city hall. Fallon called his home the "prettiest in San Jose."

Typical of the Italianate style, the Fallon House has two stories, a low pitched roof, wide overhangs, a rectangular floor plan, tall ceilings and tall windows with decorative crowns. The home still stands on the corner of San Pedro and W. St. John streets in San Jose.

By the time the transcontinental railroad pulled into Alameda, Italianate was the most popular house style in the United States. Just a year earlier in 1868, prominent Oakland physician Enoch Pardee chose this style for his home. The home still exists at 11th and Castro streets in Oakland.

Perhaps Pancoast and Severance drew inspiration from the Pardee home. Pardee, however, chose to take a step that Pancoast decided against: Pardee added the square tower—a cupola—that characterizes the Italian villa. Although Pancoast chose to dispense with the cupola, he did add a porch and wide balcony to give his family's home a personality of its own.

Other families built homes in the Italianate style in the neighborhood around the Pancoast home. In 1875, D. L. Munson chose this style for his family's home on Eagle Avenue. The Munson home is a taller, more rectangular home, reminiscent of Italianate homes found in larger cities.

Munson was a mining superintendent; he lived in the home with his wife, Mary, and son, Harry. A third Italianate-style home in the neighborhood gives a taller, more massive appearance than the Pancoast or Munson home.

The Munson and Bishop homes have distinctive Italianate features not seen in the plainer Pancoast home: a bay window, taller windows with hood moldings and brackets that define the cornice line.

Before we move on to the Second Empire style, let's have a look at the Pardee family's Italianate villa in Oakland and go on a hike through Squatter Pancoast's land. And we can't forget A.A. and Emilie Cohen's exquisite Fernside villa.

DENTIST M. F. BISHOP built this home on Clement Avenue in 1876 and lived here with his wife, Jennie, and daughter, Mary.

Field trip!

The Pardee's Italianate villa

Pardee Home Musuem
627 11th Street
Oakland, CA 94607

(510) 444-2187
www.pardeehome.org

ENOCH PARDEE BUILT this Italianate villa in 1868 for his wife, Mary, and son, George. George was elected California governor in 1902 and is best remembered as the "Earthquake Governor" for his remarkable leadership after the Great San Francisco Earthquake and Fire in 1906. The home's furnishings and collections are original and authentic, and the guided tour includes the entire house, the gardens and the carriage house.

Take a hike!

Squatter Pancoast

Alameda founders William Worthington Chipman and Gideon Aughinbaugh got more than land when they sealed their deal with Don Antonio Peralta on October 22, 1851. When they purchased the *Bolsa de Encinal,* they inherited the Don's squatters. James J. Foley inherited some of these "knights errant"—as Chipman called these land-grabbers—when he purchased 104.4 acres from Chipman and Aughinbaugh. One of these was Franklin Pancoast.

Foley accused Pancoast of squatting on the northern portion of his property. Before Foley could lift a finger, his uninvited guest had a substantial operation under-way. Imelda Merlin tells us that Chipman recorded in his diary that Foley gave Pancoast five acres in 1851 for "squatter's relinquish-ment of the rest of his land."

The 1860 federal census lists Pancoast as a farmer with real estate valued at $13,000 and a per-sonal estate worth $4,000. He had a household that included himself, his 3-year-old son, Albert, and 1-year-old daughter, Ann.

A cook and a housekeeper attended to the family. Pancoast also kept farmer Joseph Colson and ten laborers under his roof.

Four years after the 1860 census, Alfred A. Cohen's San Francisco & Alameda Railroad arrived in Alameda, its tracks bisecting Pancoast's farm.

James J. Foley's tract was divid-ed up sometime in the 1870s as crops gave way to homes. Foley Street is all that reminds us of the early property owner. In 1874 the government approved plans to connect the estuary with San Leandro Bay. When the canal was finished, water would flow right by the neighborhood. An 1875 map shows renewed interest in the real estate between the train station on Park Street and new waterway. Franklin Pancoast's farm has been reduced to the small Pancoast Tract.

Banker Levi Jenks likely part-nered with Simeon P. Meads to create the "Jenks & Meads Homestead." (Jenks was the presi-dent of the original Bank of Alameda, which opened its doors on September 7, 1878. The follow-ing October, the institution changed its name to the First National Bank of Alameda.)

Investors also put their hopes in a homestead named for the nearby Alameda Station.

As the 19th century turned to the 20th, homes and businesses began to fill the fields that Franklin Pancoast had farmed with his household. In 1902 estu-rary water began to flow along the new neighborhood.

Let's take a walk and see what's become of Franklin Pancoast's old neighborhood.

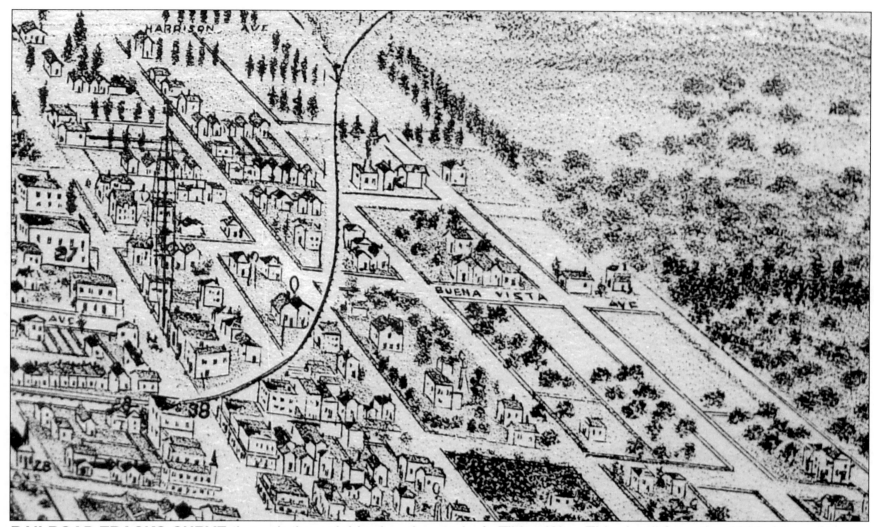

RAILROAD TRACKS CURVE through the neighborhood on today's Tilden Way. This detail from the 1888 *Alameda Argus* map shows the Southern Pacific Railroad's station on Park Street (38) with a light mast just to the north. The Central Pacific Railroad absorbed A.A. Cohen's San Francisco & Alameda Railroad in 1869. The Southern Pacific Railroad absorbed the Central Pacific the following year. Compare this map to the ones on the next page.

Our exploration of Franklin Pancoast's old farmlands starts and ends at Lincoln Avenue and Park Street. (The letters in the text refer to the letters on the map on the right.) As we start we have to imagine the old train station (A) between Tilden Way and Lincoln Avenue just to your left. Starting in 1864, trains entered Alameda on tracks whose bed later became Tilden Way.

A.A. Cohen built the first station at this spot in 1864. The Southern Pacific Railroad replaced Cohen's station in 1895.

Walk down Lincoln to Everett Street. On the right are three palm trees that define five Colonial Revival homes (B).

The unknown builder of these handsome homes spiced things up, using the classic box, the peaked gable and the Dutch gambrel roof.

Take a left on Everett and walk one block to Noble Avenue (C). This street is lined with bungalows and remembers George Noble, who was Alameda's most prolific bungalow builder. Walk along the

James J. Foley's tract was divided up sometime in the 1870s as crops gave way to homes. Foley Street is all that's left to remind us of the early property owner.

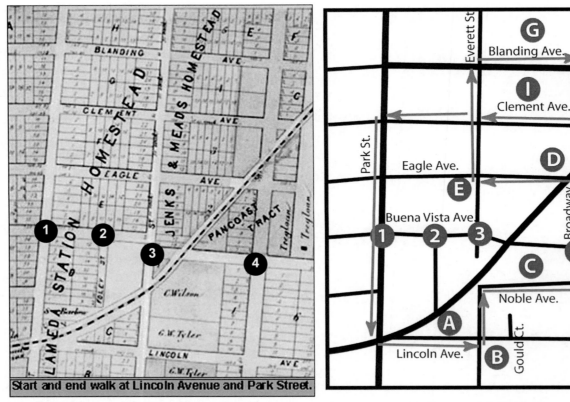

Start and end walk at Lincoln Avenue and Park Street.

NUMBERS ON EACH MAP show street intersections with Buena Vista Avenue: 1. Park Street; 2. Foley Street; 3. Everett Street; 4. Broadway. Letters refer to stops along the way. Compare these to the *Alameda Argus* map on the previous page.

bungalows until you reach the backyards of the homes along Broadway. The rear of these yards marked the property boundary between James Foley's land and property belonging to former Texas Rangers Jack Hays and John Caperton.

Hays and Caperton also owned property in today's North Oakland and Oakland's Montclair District. Hays served as San Francisco's first sheriff. In 1873, Hays and Caperton had Broadway built through their property from Central to Buena Vista avenues.

Take a left on Broadway, cross Buena Vista Avenue and walk down to Eagle Avenue. Take a left into the cul-de-sac. Notice the handsome green Italianate home here (D). This is the Munson home.

Continue down Eagle Avenue to Everett Street. Look across the street to the left and you'll see Franklin Pancoast's handsome home (E).

Levi Jenks built a more modest home for himself nearby at 2500 Everett Street. Take a right on Everett Street and walk down to Blanding Avenue. Look across Blanding; that's Oakland across the way.

Notice something on the 1875 map? Harrison Avenue is gone; sacrificed to the estuary (F).

Just across the street to the right you'll see the brick building (G) The Alameda Rug Works first did business on this spot. Then the Clamp Swing Pricing Company took over. They manufactured metal card holders that suspended (swung) the price in front of products on store shelves.

Take a right on Blanding Street and walk to the next block. Notice the sign that says "Stone Boat Yard" on the building across the street? That sign is all that remains of one of the

CAPTAIN JACK: San Francisco's first sheriff and celebrated Texas Ranger Captain Jack Hays joined fellow Texas Ranger Major John Caperton to purchase a piece of the *Bolsa de Encinal*.

area's oldest boatyards and a venerable San Francisco Bay institution. It closed its doors in 2007.

Take a right onto Broadway. (Be careful, as there's no street sign here). Look across Broadway and you'll see a row of handsome Queen Anne-style homes (H) designed and built by Joseph Leonard (of Leonardville fame) in 1890. They cost $2,500 each to build.

Take a right on Clement Avenue; here you'll see one of the area's smaller dwellings at 2531 Clement. H.N. Maybee built it in 1875. He must have been pleased; he built a similar house across the street at 2532 Clement four years later.

Just down Clement Avenue is the last house on the tour, the Italianate at 2515 (I). Dentist M. F. Bishop moved in with his wife, Jennie,and daughter, Mary, in 1876.

Continue down Clement to Park Street; go left and return to Lincoln Avenue with memories of a stroll through one of Alameda's older but lesser-known neighborhoods.

ALAMEDA'S LOST ITALIANATE VILLA: This Eadweard Muybridge photograph shows the approach to Alfred A. and Emilie Cohen's Italianate-style villa, The entrance to the estate was near the intersection of today's Versailles and Buena Vista avenues.

Fernside

A grand estate

In 1868, Alfred A. Cohen sold the majority of his stock in the Oakland Railroad and Ferry Company to the Central Pacific Railroad's Big Four: Leland Stanford, Charles Crocker, Collis Huntington and Mark Hopkins. A year later he sold the foursome the majority of his San Francisco, Alameda & Haywards Railroad stock.

In September 1869, the transcontinental railroad was set to arrive at San Francisco Bay. There was one problem; the San Francisco & Oakland Railroad's wharf at Gibbons Point was not yet ready to accommodate the trains. Cohen was happy to learn that the history-making train would arrive on "his" tracks—on the "Cohen Line."

When Cohen sold his line to the Central Pacific's Big Four, he became a wealthy man who could afford the best. In 1872, he and his wife, Emilie, hired the architectural firm of Wright and Sanders to help express their affluence.

The following year John Wright and George H. Sanders (variably spelled Saunders) completed the 70-plus-room mansion that anchored the Cohen's palatial estate. In social registers, such as the San Francisco Blue Book, the Cohens listed their residence as "Fernside, Buena Vista & Versailles Avenue, Alameda."

ALFRED A. COHEN described himself as a "horticulturalist" to the federal census taker who knocked at the door of the Cohen residence in 1860. The census taker recorded that Alfred was from England, his wife, Emilie, from Delaware; the couple's two children, Willie and Edgar, were both born in California.

The Cohens had hired no ordinary men to build their home. Five years before they submitted their design to the Cohens, Wright and Sanders had designed the State Asylum for the Deaf, Dumb and Blind in Berkeley (today's Clark Kerr Campus at the University of California).

The architects first designed a stone Gothic Revival building for the asylum. When a fire destroyed the structure in January 1875, Wright and Sanders returned to the drawing boards. They designed new buildings that included an educational building, dormitories, support facilities and a private residence for the principal. The asylum's successor, the California Schools for the Deaf and Blind, used these and other later facilities until 1980.

In 1868, Wright and Sanders won the prestigious competition to design the buildings for the University of California's new campus in Berkeley. The pair backed out when they learned the regents would not permit them to be involved in the building process, a step that would have considerably reduced their fee.

Wright and Sanders' Italianate design for the Cohens towered over Fernside. The home with all its trappings was said to have cost the staggering sum of $300,000. In *Ultimate Victorians*, Elinor Richey described the Cohens' home as, "the most splendid of all Italian villas in the East Bay." Richey says that Wright and Sanders—no doubt with some input from London-born A.A. Cohen—used Queen Victoria's summer home on the Isle of Wight as a model.

Richey describes the home as a "vast towered three-story rectangular structure with its sweeping carriage entrance and double porte-cochere." She says it "rather resembled a luxury hotel at a luxury spa." The home so impressed Hopkins that he hired Wright and Sanders to design his Nob Hill home. Crocker and Stanford included some features of the Cohen villa into their own homes.

One impressive feature: visitors could stroll through the Cohens' art gallery, which took up an entire floor, and ogle at paintings by such artists as Albert Bierstadt. Portraits of the Cohen family by Charles Nahl also graced the gallery.

THE ALAMEDA SEMI-WEEKLY ARGUS included A.A. and Emilie Cohen's Fernside mansion and carriage house on its 1888 map.

Cohen remained the president of the San Francisco, Alameda & Haywards Railroad and also served as the Central Pacific's attorney. Richey says that Cohen could scarcely abide members of the Big Four. He looked down on them as, "men whose habits, modes of thought and conversation were not calculated to advance me."

Cohen often clashed with these men, once over how they forced him to leave his private rail car in an out-of-the-way place in the railyards. He resigned as counsel in 1876 in protest over what he called unfair tariffs and practices. He advocated the first bill in California to regulate freight rates.

A.A. Cohen died on Nov. 6, 1887, aboard his private railroad car near Sydney, Nebraska. He was on his way home from New York. He was laid to rest at Oakland's Mountain View Cemetery.

On March 23, 1897, the *New York Times* reported the Cohen family's second devastating loss in 10 years: the fire that destroyed Fernside.

"The handsome residence of the late A.A. Cohen was destroyed by fire from a defective flue," the *Times* told its readers. "The house was filled with elegant furniture and works of art. Many of the pictures in the art gallery had been bought in Europe, and represented a large outlay."

Emilie remained at Fernside after the fire, moving into a less-elegant building on the estate grounds. She had survived the death of her husband; now she survived the fire. When Emilie died in 1925, the children subdivided the estate and sold land to developers south of a boundary line that became Fernside Boulevard. All that's left to remind us of the grand estate's existence in Alameda is the neighborhood's name that echoes its grandeur, "Fernside."

Details, details!

Italianate

HERE'S WHAT TO LOOK FOR:

1. Asymmetrical shapes to imitate the sprawling look of an Italian villa

2. Low-pitched, often flat roofs

3. Bay windows

4. Windows with heavy hoods or elaborate surrounds

5. Quoins: Woodwork that imitates stonework on the building's corners

6. Façade rises above the roofline, called a "false front"

7. Heavy, often elaborately carved supporting brackets under the eaves.

THERE WERE NO RULE BOOKS. Not all Italianate houses had all the elements noted here. For example, the house pictured here is symmetrical, rather than assymmetrical, and the supporting brackets are light, rather than heavy. Did you notice the false front? Read more about this home on pages 107 and 108.

Second Empire

Progress was kind to Patrick and Ann Britt. In the 1870s, they were supporting themselves and their four children, Ellie, Pat, George and Mattie, on a farm in Alameda's West End—a place historian Woody Minor calls a "hinterland, a wind-swept forest encompassed by marshland and bay." Alameda County built a bridge on the other side of the peninsula in 1871, which crossed the estuary at Webster Street. Minor says the bridge brought a "true end to isolation" and provided easier access to the city of Oakland. The following summer the city opened Webster Street, which led directly to the Britts' farm.

Then in 1878, James Fair—known as "Slippery Jim" or "Sunny Jim," depending on your point of view—and Alfred "Hog" Davis began running their South Pacific Coast trains on Central Avenue right along the Britts' property.

The following spring, the Britts sold their bucolic seven-acre spread for the lofty sum of $21,000; the buyers transformed the farm into Long Branch Baths. Pat and Ann spent $6,000 of their profits to build a handsome hotel in the Second Empire style right where the South Pacific Coast Railroad tracks intersected Webster Street. They named it the Britt Hotel.

The 1880 federal census tells us that the Britt family had grown from four to nine children and now included Martha, Mary, Loretta, Willie and Richard. Pat—as he was known to

AFTER THE ACCIDENT: Bicyclists gather at Crolls sometime after a train explosion on July 15, 1903, blew out the building's windows. The signs "Real Estate Building" and "Real Estate" (highlighted) are from Alameda builder A. R. Denke's office, which was in the building at the time of the accident. The signs are also visible in the later photograph on the previous page, but the words "Real Estate Building" are gone from the larger sign.

Did you notice?

The builder designed the Britt Hotel's balcony to accommodate the telegraph poles, which were there first. The American District Telegraph Company of Alameda erected them in 1877, two years before the Britts built their hotel and one year before the South Pacific Coast Railroad began running on Central Avenue.

his friends—and Ann needed more income to support such a large family. They realized that they were in the right place at the right time to do so.

Minor says that the Britt Hotel remained the costliest building on Webster Street for years to come. In 1885, the SPCRR obligingly built a station on Webster Street at the hotel's front door.

In 1891, the Croll family bought the hotel and lent the building the name we call it today: Croll's, which is both an Alameda Historical Monument and a California State Historical Landmark.

"This building is closely associated with sporting events significant to the history of the City of Alameda, the San Francisco Bay Area and the State of California," says the state landmark plaque. "Croll's is important in the early development of boxing during the Golden Age of Boxing in California, a period of great California champions such as Jim Corbett and James Jeffries."

The other end of town

In 1880, just one year after the Britts opened their hotel at Central Avenue and Webster Street, Adolph H. Schnabel hired Edward Childs to build a home in the Second Empire Style for him at 2233 Santa Clara Avenue close to Park Street.

The 1880 census, taken in June, shows Adolph and his brother Augustus living in Otto Beck's hotel on Montgomery Street in San Francisco. Both the census and the home's documents list Adolph Schnabel as a mining expert.

In 1889, a third dwelling in the Second Empire style appeared on Alameda's landscape, this one a cottage on Encinal Avenue. Julius Remmel of the building and real estate firm of Marcuse & Remmel originally owned this home, pictured on page 69.

The Britt Hotel, Adolph Schnabel's house and a Julius Remmel cottage all have something in common. They each sport the mansard roof of the Second Empire style, which became popular in the 1850s in France. The style's signature roof appeared all over Great Britain and the United States as other architects followed the French lead.

THIS DETAIL FROM the 1888 *Alameda Semi-Weekly Argus* map shows the two-story Mansard-style Britt Hotel at the intersection of Webster Street and Central Avenue. The South Pacific Coast Railroad tracks are visible on Central Avenue near the hotel as are the Long Branch Baths along the bay shore.

EDWARD CHILDS built this home in 1880 for Adolph Schnabel. The design combines elements of the Italianate style with the Second Empire style's mansard roof. It is known today as "The Mansard Building."

Along with this roof, homes in the Second Empire style, like the one at 2233 Santa Clara Avenue, also have an Italianate (or Stick-style) flavor with square decorative window crowns, brackets and single-story porches. The pipettes on the bay windows give the Schnabel home has an unmistakable Italianate appearance. Remmel's cottage has a Stick-style bay window and fish-scale shingles that anticipate the Queen Anne style.

It's the mansard roof that really sets these three buildings apart. François Mansart, for whom the roof is named, was born is 1598 in Paris. Mansart did not invent the roof, but perfected it and widely used it to crown his creations.

He began with a hip roof and added dormers. As time went on, Mansart gave his eponymous roof two pitches—a flatter pitch on top, and a much steeper pitch on the sides.

Mansart worked as a master carpenter, stonemason and sculptor. He began studying architecture in his early 20s. He was such a perfectionist that he would sometimes tear down his own buildings and start over. Consequently only the wealthiest patrons could afford to work with him. The only surviving example of his early work is the chateau of Balleroy. The best preserved example of his mature style is the chateau of Maisons-Laffitte.

When Louis XIV became king in 1643, Mansart lost many of his commissions to other architects. For example, he had commissions to redesign the Louvre and the royal mausoleum at Saint-Denis; neither was executed.

The Second Empire style became very popular because Mansart's roof efficiently allowed complete use of a building's top floor. This feature may have attracted Pat and Ann Britt, as the mansard roof allowed more space for hotel rooms and the revenue they would generate.

At the same time the Britts were building their hotel, architects and builders had already turned to the more austere "Stick" style, the subject of our next chapter.

Field trip!

Sacramento's Old Governor's Mansion

Governor's Mansion State Historic Park
1526 H Street
Sacramento, CA 95814

(916) 323-3047
There is an admission price.

ALBERT AND CLEMENZA GALLATIN were the orginal owners of this 1877 Second Empire jewel. The state of California purchased the home in 1903 for $25,000. Gov. George Pardee was the first to live here as governor with his family. The Pardee family's Oakland home is the subject of the field trip on page 55. Twelve other California governors including Earl Warren and Ronald Reagan lived in this home whose tower even has the signature mansard roof.

Details, details!

Second Empire

HERE'S WHAT TO LOOK FOR:

1. Steep mansard roof

2. Dormer windows with elaborate details

3. Colored roof shingles

4. Decorative ornament along the top of the roof called "cresting"

THERE WERE NO RULE BOOKS. Not all Second Empire houses had all the elements noted here. For example, the cottage pictured here has no cresting. (Croll's Hotel on page 64 has this decorative ornament along part of its roofline.) This Second Empire cottage has a Stick-style bay window and fish-scale shingles normally found on Queen Anne-style homes. Did you notice the fanciful bow surrounding the home's entryway?

POLLEN CUNNINGHAM, the superintendent at the California Planing Mill, built this Stick-style home in the Gold Coast neighborhood in 1878. Four years later he sold it to J. R. Spring. The home's brackets, braces, gabled roof and clapboard wall surface are all elements of the Stick style.

Stick style

In 1868, architects William Hoagland and John J. Newsom built an Italianate-style villa for Enoch Pardee at 11th and Castro streets in Oakland. Although they constructed the home using redwood, the architects wanted it to look as though they had built the home with stone.

They added quoins to the sides of the structure and ordered carefully mixed paint the texture of stone. One story says that Pardee himself supervised the mixing of the colors. He did not want his villa to look like it was made of wood. Pardee wanted the painters to produce a color that would belie the fine elegance of stone, even though his architects had not included a single stone in their plans.

That same year, architect Henry Hobson Richardson took the opposite tack on the East Coast when he built a home for himself and his family at Arrochair on Staten Island. Unlike Hoagland and Newsom, Richardson clothed his house in clapboard, leaving no mistake that he had designed and built the family residence in wood.

ARCHITECT GEORGE A. BORDWELL designed this Stick-style villa on Pacific Avenue for real estate investor William T.S. Ryer and his wife, Mary, in 1886. Ryer worked in San Francisco. In 1885, a year before he built the Ryer home, Bordwell designed the buildings at 1430-40 Park Street.

Richardson used wood with no attempt at disguise. In doing so, the renowned architect had tapped into Andrew Jackson Downing's philosophy of leaving wood unveiled and thus emphasizing what Vincent Scully calls its truth and reality.

"This (philosophy) was always given to structural and visual multiplication of the framing sticks," says Scully, who coined the term "Stick style" in his 1955 book *The Shingle Style and the Stick Style*. In their time, these homes were called "modern" with words like Gothic, Swiss or English cottage used to describe the design inspiration. The Stick style grew from Downing's Picturesque Gothic ideals and flourished in house pattern books. Its proponents

THIS PAIR OF VICTORIAN-ERA COTTAGES on Park Avenue reflects the Stick style with their squared bay windows and decorative barge boards.

lauded the style's structural honesty. In *A Field Guide to American Houses*, Virginia and Lee McAlester point out, however, that "the applied stickwork, unlike true half-timbering, had no structural relation to the underlying balloon-frame construction."

The McAlesters identify three types of Stick-style houses: gabled roof, towered and townhouse. Each of these types had appeared in Alameda by the mid-1880s, when this "modern" style had gained popularity. In 1885 Robert Smilie built a pair of gabled cottages on Park Avenue. Two years later, Robert Harvey built a two-story town house in the style just across the street. In the year between, San Francisco real estate nabob W.T.S. Ryer hired architect George A. Bordwell to design a towered villa in the new style on Pacific Avenue.

The McAlesters say that decorative detailing—evident on Alameda's Stick-style homes—defines the style, whether with "characteristic multi-textured wall surfaces" or with "roof trusses whose stickwork faintly mimics the exposed members of medieval half-timbered houses." Unlike the wooden elements that builders of Italianate style home shaped to resemble stone, the Stick style builders shaped porch posts, brackets and other support beams square with beveled edges.

The Stick style's patterns and lines prevailed over the three-dimensional ornamentation found on Italianate-style buildings. The Corinthian columns with their pronounced acanthus leaves were gone. Fancy brackets beneath the cornice line gave way to plainer supports.

Stick-style homes featured wood siding, steep gabled roofs, overhanging eaves, ornamental trusses, decorative braces and brackets, and decorative half-timbering.

Architects and builders dressed some Stick-style architecture using ideas borrowed from Queen Victoria's furniture designer Charles Eastlake. In the same year that Hoagland and Newsom designed the Pardee home and Richardson was busy building his family's home, Eastlake published *Hints on Household Taste in Furniture, Upholstery, and Other Details.* In the book Eastlake favored hand-made furniture and decor or those made by machine workers who took personal pride in their work. This book was so popular that it went through six editions in the next 11 years.

Manufacturers in the United States used Eastlake's drawings and ideas to make Eastlake Style or Cottage furniture. Eastlake designed furniture with geometric ornaments, spindles, low relief carvings and incised lines. Eastlake felt that builders took his ideas beyond the pale when they applied his furniture designs to the exteriors of homes. Robert Smilie included Eastlake sunbursts on his Park Avenue cottages; Robert Harvey also includes Eastlake designs on this home across the street.

Some refer to the Stick style as the Eastlake style. But other than lending his spindles, sunbursts, flowers, comets and other fanciful designs to both the Stick and Queen Anne styles, Eastlake had little to do with these architectural styles. He often disavowed the use of his name to describe anything other than his own furniture designs.

According to the McAlesters, the Stick style links the Gothic Revival with the Queen Anne style. "All three styles are free adaptations of medieval English building traditions," the authors say. Unlike the earlier Gothic Revival style, however, the Stick style "stressed the wall surfaces as a decorative element rather than as a plane." This decorative element applied to the wall surfaces strongly influenced the Queen Anne style that replaced the Stick style.

ROBERT HARVEY BUILT his Park Avenue home in the "modern" style adding squared bay windows and dressing the home in geometric ornaments. The gable's fish-scale shingles anticipate the Queen Anne style.

Field trip!

Oakland Stick-style home has Alameda connections

Cohen-Bray House
1440 29th Avenue
Oakland, CA 94601

(510) 536-1703
www.cohen-brayhouse.info
There is an admission fee.

The Cohen-Bray House: Watson A. Bray and his wife, Julia, began building this Stick-style home in 1882 for their daughter Emma. The Brays were anticipating Emma's marriage to attorney Alfred H. Cohen, which took place on February 28, 1884.

Emma's spouse was the son of Emilie and A.A. Cohen, the latter also a lawyer. Both families were socially prominent and well-to-do. Bray was a successful commodities broker; A.A. Cohen, an attorney for the Central Pacific Railroad. (Read more about the Cohens on pages 60 to 62.)

The Brays bought the land and built the house. The senior Cohens completely furnished the home ahead of time. This allowed the bride and groom to move in on their wedding day after a lavish ceremony at Oak Tree Farm, the Bray mansion that once stood directly across the street. The home is a quintessential example of the Stick style, and retains much of its original furnishing. The house has never been sold out of the family; Emma and Alfred's descendents continue to live in the house.

Details, details!

Stick style

HERE'S WHAT TO LOOK FOR:

1. "Sticks," flat board banding and geometric ornamentation; patterns and lines rather than three-dimensional ornamentation

2. Clapboard wall surface

3. Rectangular shape

4. Steep, gabled roof

5. Overhanging eaves

6. Decorative braces and brackets

THERE WERE NO RULE BOOKS. Not all Stick-style houses had all the elements noted here, for example, the house pictured here is asymmetrical, rather than rectangular. Notice the cresting along the roofline.

IN 1890 Travelers Insurance agent Walter W. Haskell hired architect Charles Shaner to design this classic Queen Anne-style home. Pioneer Alameda builder Dennis Straub executed Shaner's design. Haskell lived here with his wife, Clara, and daughter, Vora.

Queen Anne

The United States celebrated its 100th birthday with the Philadelphia Centennial Exposition, which displayed new technologies on the ground's 13 acres. The workings of the 1400-horsepower steam engine no doubt mesmerized visitors. The George H. Corliss Co. designed the engine to power exhibits like Charles Brush's electric lights and the Otis Brothers' elevators.

Exposition-goers gazed at locomotives, fire trucks, printing presses and mining equipment. They gathered around the latest inventions—some that we take for granted today. Christopher Sholes and Carlos Glidden displayed their typewriter with something many of us struggle with even in the digital age—Sholes' QWERTY keyboard.

Alexander Graham Bell's fledgling company demonstrated the inventor's telephone. George Bernard Grant proudly exhibited his 12 x 6-inch calculator with its 400 moving parts. You could order one at the exposition, but at $1,000 it was a rich man's toy.

English architect Richard Norman Shaw used the exposition to introduce an architectural style that he called "Queen Anne" because he thought that it mirrored styles prominent in the early

A.W. PATTIANI designed and built this Queen Anne-style home on Union Street for San Francisco commission merchant Alonzo Fink in 1890. Fink paid Pattiani the handsome sum of $5,200. He lived in the home with his wife, May, and daughter, Alison.

18th century. Although many question Shaw's sketchy connection, the name has stood the test of time. The Victorian-era Queen Anne style had little to do with the British monarch who ruled Great Britain and Ireland from 1702 to 1714, however.

Widely published pattern books like George F. Barber's *The Cottage Souvenir Revised and Enlarged* touted spindles and other flourishes we associate with the Queen Anne style today. The style appealed to everyone: country folk who yearned for fancy city trappings and city dwellers who pulled out all the stops as they built lavish castles using Shaw's ideas and Barber's interpretation of them.

Architects combined conical towers, multiple gables and contrasting shingle patterns to create an elaborate, multifaceted architecture, according to Kristin Holmes and David Watersun in *The Victorian Express*.

In *A Field Guide to American Homes,* Virginia and Lee McAlester divide the Queen Anne style into four types: patterned masonry, free classic, half-timbered and spindled. Spindled is the style we most frequently think of when we hear the term "Queen Anne." These "gingerbread" houses boasted delicate turned porch posts and lacy, ornamental spindles. Some decoration on the homes, like sunbursts and meteors, is often called Eastlake because it resembles the work of English furniture designer Charles Eastlake.

The salient elements of Queen Anne-style homes also included angled bay windows and sometimes a tower or turret. (A turret is simply a tower without its own foundation.) The style reached its height of popularity with the open, spacious porch, one of its most striking features. Many Queen Anne homes boast classic porches adorned with gingerbread trim, brackets, ornate spindles and spandrels, intricately sawn wooden balusters, fluted columns and turned and painted posts.

A reliable delivery system played an important role in Alameda's real estate development. Both the Central Pacific (called the Southern Pacific after 1885) and the South Pacific Coast railroads made affordable, mass-produced doors, windows, roofing, siding and decorative detailing more readily available. Architects and builders like A.W. Pattiani and Joseph Leonard took full advantage of this system and helped dress Alameda in the Queen Anne splendor the Island City is still famous for.

GEORGE H. CORLISS CO. designed the engine that powered all the exhibits in Machinery Hall at the 1876 Philadelphia Centennial Exposition. Corliss's masterpiece spun a 56-ton flywheel to produce 1400 horsepower. The engine embodied 19th century technology.

Gingerbread: Tasty to some, indigestible to others

Author Richard Henry Dana sailed home from San Diego aboard the *Alert*. When he later described the ship in *Two Years Before the Mast*, he used the word "gingerbread" with some disdain.

"There was no foolish gilding and gingerbread work to take the eye of landsmen and passengers, but everything was ship-shape and Bristol fashion," he wrote.

Put the gilt on the gingerbread

Dana was by no means coining a phrase with his 1836 description. Sailors in the British Navy first used the term "gingerbread" or "gingerwork" in the middle of the 18th century to refer to the gilded decoration on their ships. "The gilt on the gingerbread" referred to the fine gilding on the carvings—the gingerbread—around a ship's stern and along its quarter galleries. "Put the gilding on the gingerbread" entered the English language as a maritime expression—similar to today's "put the icing on the cake."

Gilt served as a mark of a captain's wealth and his success at taking prizes. Carvings painted in cheap dockyard yellow, on the other hand, often signified a less successful or less-than-generous captain.

"A warm welcome greets us as we enter. The furniture within is in keeping with things without; nothing is tawdry; there is no gingerbread gilding; all is handsome

DISPLAY OF WEALTH: The decoration on the stern of the Royal Dutch India ship *Amsterdam* served to convince onlookers that her owner prospered. Such decoration, called gingerwork or gingerbread, had its detractors.

Gingerbread began to adorn Victorian-era homes with the wooden "icicle" bargeboards of the Gothic Revival style. "Icicles" dripped from William Tecumseh Sherman's home in San Francisco when he lived there in the 1850s

A GILDED SUNBURST joins the decorated bargeboard, fish-scale shingles, cresting and a finial to round out this home's Queen Anne-style gingerbread.

and substantial," wrote Mary Boykin Chestnut during the Civil War in *A Diary from Dixie.*

Chestnut's words leave no doubt that by the Civil War, "gingerbread" had made its way from maritime into mainstream English to mean any gaudy—and to some—tasteless ornamentation. Members in Chestnut's polite circle regarded "gingerbread" as something tawdry, the despised antonym of "handsome and substantial."

(Chestnut's name may strike a familiar chord. Filmmaker Ken Burns relied heavily on her diary when he made his public television documentary about the Civil War.)

Dripping bargeboards

Not everyone agreed with Dana and Chestnut, however. Gingerbread began to adorn Victorian-era homes with the wooden "icicle" bargeboards of the Gothic Revival style. "Icicles" dripped from William Tecumseh Sherman's home in San Francisco when he lived there in the 1850s as a banker.

When the "Carpenter Gothic" style arose in response to a growing demand for housing, imagination took over with an explosion of details that culminated in the Queen Anne style 30 years later when overactive imaginations led to mass-produced wooden sunbursts, comets, flowers, lace and more.

By the 1880s, architects, designers and homeowners were ready for the gilding that Dana and Chestnut abhorred.

Richard Norman Shaw introduced America to the Queen Anne style, the style most people associate with gingerbread, at the 1876 Centennial Exposition in Philadelphia, where the British government constructed several buildings highlighting "Queen Anne."

Shaw's style, with its requisite gingerbread, rules Alameda's Victorian-era architectural scene boasting turrets, towers, brackets, spandrels and fish-scale shingles.

Gingerbread *extraordinaire*

No home bespeaks the Queen Anne style more forcefully than David Brehaut's home on San Jose Avenue, pictured on the right.

Architect and builder David S. Brehaut made a bold statement in gingerbread when he built his San Jose Avenue home in 1893.

Brehaut teamed up with fellow Alameda architect and builder Charles S. Shaner; together they graced the street with what Alameda Historical Museum Curator George C. Gunn calls a real "tour-de-force."

Brehaut and Shaner presented the home as what Gunn called a "salesman's sample." Brehaut wanted to showcase his skills to prospective clients. The result: an elaborately striking, ornately decorated Queen Anne-style home all dressed in gingerbread.

According to Kenneth Naversen in *West Coast Victorians: A Nineteenth Century Legacy*, Shaner based the house on pattern-book Design No. 27 in George F. Barber's *The Cottage Souvenir Revised and Enlarged*.

George Franklin Barber was a Tennessee architect who enjoyed considerable influence especially in the South and Midwest. Barber produced a number of popular house-pattern books, which made him something of an arbiter of architectural taste in America.

"The central tower and dual entry porch with its open pavilion are elements of (Barber's) plan," says Naversen, "while the more or less symmetrical wings

GINGERBREAD was on the menu when Alameda builder David S. Brehaut partnered with architect Charles S. Shaner to design and build Brehaut's home on San Jose Avenue. Brehaut and Shaner freely borrowed from one of Tennessee architect George S. Barber's designs, shown on the right.

The home boasts a grand tower complete with the "gingerbread" wealthy 19th-century capitalists had come to expect. A wonder-filled gable speaks to the street with decoration concentrated on the bargeboards.

are Shaner's contribution—unless, of course, they too derive from a stock-design source."

"The incised boxed newel posts and odd keystone-shaped windows are certainly Shaner's contributions," says Gunn.

The home boasts a grand tower complete with the "gingerbread" embellishments wealthy 19th-century capitalists had come to expect. The eye is drawn to the unusual finial atop the tower that does not bring the usual "witch's cap" to mind, but emphasizes the home's uniqueness.

The builders took a page from Barber's design, and even crowned the porch with its own miniature tower complete with a golden finial. Spindles and columns

draw the eye around the front of this late Victorian-era showpiece.

A wonder-filled gable speaks to the street with its over-abundance of gingerbread decoration concentrated on the bargeboards. Brehaut and Shaner capped the gable's finial with an unusual bowl. In another small touch, they varied from Barber's design and shaped the spindles on the upstairs porch blending them with a wheel or flower motif.

Many other Alameda architects and builders applied gingerbread dressing to their designs, but none as fancifully as Brehaut affixed to his San Jose Avenue Queen Anne-style masterwork.

Innovation

The indespensible scroll saw

Brackets and corbels, finials and drops, spandrels and running trim: all these are integral parts of the Victorian-era architectural landscape and none would have been possible without the scroll saw.

The scroll saw, or something akin to it, has been with us for hundreds of years. Hand-held coping saws and fretsaws had performed similar tasks since the Middle Ages. The need to apply fancy wooden designs—from the icicle bargeboards that graced Gothic Revival homes to the fancier trim on Queen Anne residences—increased the demand for the versatile scroll saw and inspired inventors to improve on ancient hand-held devices.

In 1863 William Doane applied for a patent for a "scroll saw mill"; over the next 10 years, he applied for seven more patents for this device. He was not alone; by 1873 Henry Bickford, William Dobson and Isaac Hird also applied for scroll saw patents. Numerous other inventors applied for ancillary patents for scroll saw blades, blade holders, blade-aligning devices, tables, adjusting wrenches and more.

And akin to building the proverbial better mousetrap, work continues today on improving the scroll saw. In February 2008, an inventor applied for United States Patent 7,328,514. He told the Patent Office that his "Power Tool Bearing Arrangement" is a better way to keep the scroll saw blade steady. In March 2008 another inventor applied for United States Patent 7,359,762. This device offers the scroll saw user the ability to interface with a computer.

SCROLL SAW NO. 7: The W. F. and John Barnes Company designed this tool to allow carpenters to precisely cut architectural embellishments.

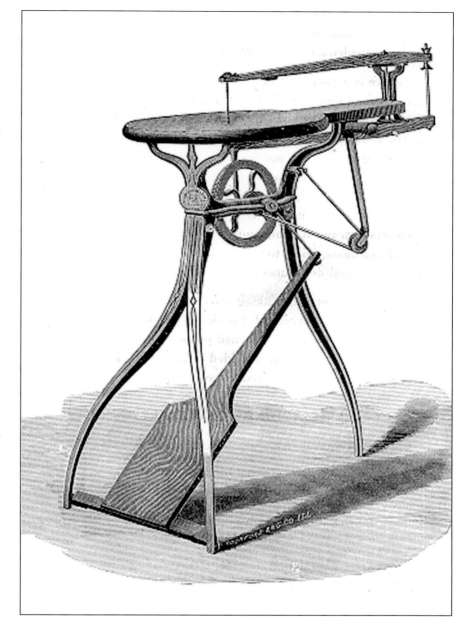

From Victorian times people have confused jigsaws with scroll saws. A jigsaw—so called because people thought the blade was dancing a jig—is a hand-held tool with which you guide the blade as it cuts the wood. The scroll saw, on the other hand, has a table on which you guide the wood as the blade cuts through it. In 1873 Marvin E. Weller patented "an improvement in jigsaws." A close look at his patent reveals that Weller's invention has a table; he was not improving the jigsaw, but the scroll saw. I found an article written in 2007 in which a physics teacher describes a scroll saw as a "jigsaw with a table," so the confusion continues to this day.

Inventors saw the inefficiency of hand-held saws when it came to cutting the intricate designs that 19th century architecture demanded. They turned to an unlikely source for inspiration: the sewing machine. Why not design a saw that could glide through wood like a sewing machine needle glides through fabric? Why not let the saw blade do the work the way a sewing machine needle does? Why not lay the wood on a table as you do with fabric on a sewing machine?

Like saws, machines for sewing had been around for generations; sewing machines evolved from the hand-held needle. Then in 1790 Thomas Saint sketched a prototype of a machine that would punch a hole in leather and guide thread into the hole. Attempts to perfect the sewing machine by Thomas Stone and James Henderson in 1804, by Balthasar Krems in 1810, by Josef Madersperger in 1814 and by John Adams Doge and John Knowles in 1818 all failed and were soon forgotten by the public.

Finally in 1834, two inventors whose names are still familiar to us entered the fray: Elias Howe and Isaac Singer. The machine in Howe's patent was hand-powered and the needle moved from side to side. Singer hit on the idea that inspired the scroll saw: his machine was powered by a foot treadle and the needle moved up and down. All the early scroll saws borrowed these two ideas.

One of the premier American scroll saw manufacturers during the Victorian era was the W.F. & John Barnes Company in Rockford, Illinois. The company was organized in 1868 by two brothers: William Fletcher Barnes was a model maker, John Barnes an inventor.

The brothers extolled simplicity and poked fun at unnecessary complications. "We frequently find in our correspondence parties who seem to think that by use of heavy balance wheels and complicated devices there will be generated, in some mysterious way, more power than resides in the operator himself," the company said in its 1885 catalog. "This is impossible; all that can be done is to use in the most direct and effective manner the power that exists."

That power existed in the human frame and was applied by the leg and foot to the company's Scroll Saw No. 7. "This machine is designed for practical service in the workshops of carpenters and builders, cabinet makers and other wood workers," the catalog said. "We warrant it to be well made, of good material and workmanship."

The catalog promised that the Scroll Saw No. 7 "leaves the work as smooth as it is possible for any saw to do." The table and arms were made of hard maple, the frame of cast iron—strong, yet light. The 55-pound machine weighed a portable 80 pounds and was boxed, ready for shipment. The company included 1 dozen blades with each machine; all this for an affordable $15.

Scroll saws like the ones the W.F & John Barnes Company sold allowed the Victorian-era landscape to evolve as it did. The scroll saw played a very large role upon the stage of Victorian-era architecture and design. After all, what would Alameda's Webster House be without its icicle bargeboard? And how could the Brehaut House sparkle without its gingerbread?

Details, details!

Queen Anne style

HERE'S WHAT TO LOOK FOR:

1. Asymmetrical shape

2. A one-story porch that extends across one or two sides of the house

3. Turrets or towers: a turret is a tower without a foundation; a turret seems to dangle from the side of the house, while a tower is firmly rooted in the earth

4. Surfaces textured with decorative (fish-scale) shingles, patterned masonry, or half-timbering

5. Ornamental spindles and brackets

THERE WERE NO RULE BOOKS. Not all Queen Anne-style houses had all the elements noted here. The Joseph Leonard creation pictured here, however, seems to have it all, from chimney to palm tree. Did you notice that Leonard "pierced" the tower to form an upstairs porch?

Colonial Revival style

In designing these Gold Coast homes Fulller Claflin and A. W. Pattiani turned to a style that harkened back to colonial America.

In the 1890s, the residents of Alameda witnessed a pair of stately Colonial Revival-style homes rising up in the Gold Coast neighborhood.

Joseph A. Leonard was building the first—pictured on page 86—as an investment property for William Thompson (W.T.) Garratt Jr., the scion and heir of the turn-of-the-century bell-and-brass foundry owner William Thompson (W.T.) Garratt Sr.

When the senior Garratt died January, 14, 1890, he left $200,000— a sizable sum in those days—to his 21-year-old son. The young man decided to invest $16,000 of his inheritance in the speculative real estate market in Alameda. He bought property at Union and Clinton streets, just a block from San Francisco Bay.

He then hired noted San Francisco architect Fuller Claflin to design and Leonard to build the home,. Alameda Museum curator George Gunn says that Claflin was staying just a few blocks away on Paru Street with his sister-in-law, Mrs. A.H. Ward. Perhaps the Moorish villa that Claflin had designed for the Wards there had impressed Garratt and led to his granting Claflin the commission.

In 1895, A.W. Pattiani & Company built a home on Grand Street for Joseph Mallon and his wife, Teresa. This home shows how well the architect and builder understood the first Victorian-era style fully rooted in American soil.

Pattiani built the home as a "Classic Box." A Palladian-like dormer with Classic elements—a pediment, swags and pillars — draws the eye to the home's hipped roof. Pattiani added dentil-like supports at the cornice line. He then repeated the pillared theme on the home's second-story windows.

Pilasters set off each corner of the home's façade. Pattiani replicated the pilasters at the large front window and the front door. Bay windows—a carryover from the Italianate, Stick and Queen Anne styles—hint at the Victorian era when the home was built.

In designing these homes both Claflin and Pattiani had turned to a style that harkened back to colonial America and one that saw a revival with the 1876 Philadelphia Centennial Exposition. This celebration of America's 100th birthday inspired a new interest in domestic architecture. Many of the buildings designed for the exposition were based on historically significant colonial designs.

At the same time movements were afoot to restore Boston's Old South Church and George Washington's home at Mount Vernon. A series of articles that focused on New England's early architecture appeared in *American Architect* and *Harpers*. The publicity helped spread its popularity throughout the country.

Charles McKim, William Rutherford Mead and Stanford White—who soon formed the prominent architectural firm McKim, Mead and White—toured New England's historic towns.

"They put their field notes to good use, drawing on first-hand knowledge of architectural details and forms to produce buildings which, while totally original, rang true to an earlier design spirit," say James C. Massey and Shirley Maxwell in an article they wrote for *Old House Journal*. "Even more importantly, they published books of their drawings, spreading the Colonial Revival message across the nation."

Some credit the architectural firm of McKim, Mead and White with launching the style, which in the early phase remained the exclusive domain of their wealthy clients. The firm borrowed heavily from early American architecture. They combined various Colonial styles and contemporary elements.

Generally the Colonial Revival house is larger than its Colonial counterpart—this can certainly be said of the Garratt Mansion—and some of the individual elements are exaggerated or out of proportion with other parts of the house.

Early Colonial styles called Georgian—for British kings George I, III and III—and Adams—for architects Robert and James Adams—were prevalent in the New England colonies and form the backbone of the revival. Some architects faithfully returned to the Georgian and Adam styles. They designed Colonial Revival homes with such historical accuracy that they are difficult to distinguish from original houses. Characteristics of the Colonial Revival style include a large portico entrance, a hipped roof, dormers, Palladian windows and decorative elements like swags and urns.

The Colonial Revival style blossomed into a movement and continued in popularity well after Claflin and Pattiani designed and built their Gold Coast homes. The style echoed in Philadelphia a second time with the 1898 restoration of Independence Hall. The movement is particularly noteworthy as architects restored other historically significant homes under its aegis.

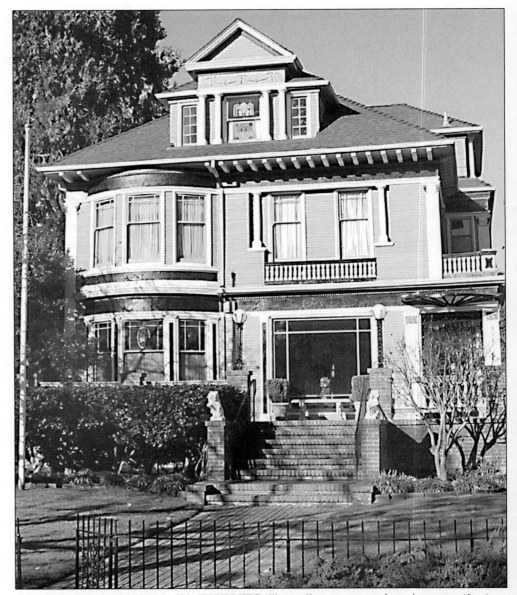

COLONIAL REVIVAL ELEMENTS like pilasters and a dormer that echoes a Palladian window adorn A.W. Pattiani's creation in Alameda's Gold Coast neighborhood.

Field trip

Meyers House & Gardens

In 1897 noted Bay Area architect Henry H. Meyers designed and built a gracious Colonial Revival-style home as his family residence. Completed at a cost of $4,000—a respectable sum for the time—the house features an elegant rounded bay window and a formal porch supported by classical columns. The interior is notable for its varnished staircase, golden oak dining room and double-size parlor.

Meyers designed dozens of buildings in the Bay Area between the 1880s and 1890s, including seven residences, two commercial buildings and two Alameda churches.

The architect's three daughters, Mildred, Edith and Jeanette, donated the residence to the city for a museum. The Alameda Museum and the Alameda Recreation and Park Department jointly manage the house and garden.

Under the direction of curator George Gunn, a band of avid Museum volunteers has outfitted the house to create the feeling of a domestic interior of the late 19th and early 20th centuries.

The Meyers House & Gardens
2021 Alameda Avenue
Alameda, CA 94501
(510) 521-1247
www.alamedamuseum.org/meyers.html
meyershouse@netscape.net

Open the fourth Saturday of every month
1 to 4 p.m.
There is an admission fee.

Remember that opening times and admission prices are subject to change. It's always wise to call ahead and check before embarking on a field trip.

Variations on a theme

A TRIO OF MATURE palm trees mark this row of Colonial Revival-style homes on Everett Street. The gambrel roof on the far left home defines it as Dutch Colonial. The steeply pitched roofs on the two homes lend them distinction as High Peaked Colonial Revival homes. Tucked into the trees to the right of this pair stands a Classic Box. Another High Peaked affair stands out of the picture to the right. All these homes were built in 1899. Get a first-hand view of these jewels on the "Squatter Pancoast" walking tour on pages 56 to 59.

Details, details!

Colonial Revival

HERE'S WHAT TO LOOK FOR:

1. Symmetrical facade

2. Pillars and columns

3. Palladian windows

4. Multi-pane, double-hung windows with shutters

5. Dormers

6. Temple-like entrance: porticos topped by balustrades

7. Simple, classical detailing

THERE WERE NO RULE BOOKS. Not all Colonial Revival houses had all the elements noted here. For example the house pictured here has double-hung windows, but no shutters. David Brehaut built this Paru Street home in 1896 for the Duveneck family, who paid the princely sum of $4,685.

JOSEPH LEONARD chose to clad his Queen Anne-style home not in gingerbread, but in brown shingles. The home once had an attic beneath a roof between the two towers. When the fire department was called to help remove the roof, a rumor began to spread that there had been a fire—a rumor that is still believed today.

Shingle style

The term "Shingle style" did not enter the architectural vocabulary until Yale professor of architecture Vincent Scully coined it in 1955.

Author Jackie Craven sees it as a rebellion, plain and simple. "Architects rebelled against Victorian fussiness when they designed rustic Shingle-style homes," she writes.

While its popularity is rooted in the same Philadelphia Centennial Exposition that introduced the gaudier Queen Anne style, the Shingle style does not stand on ceremony. Architects designed and built these homes to fit into the landscape of wooded lots, Craven says.

"Wide, shady porches encourage lazy afternoons in rocking chairs. The rough-hewn siding and the rambling shape suggest that the house was thrown together without fuss or fanfare," she writes.

Victorian-era builders had been using shingles as just one more design element, shaping them like fish scales, painting them to match the decor and surrounding them with gingerbread. Then prominent East Coast architects like Henry Hobson Richardson, Charles McKim and Stanford White began to experiment with shingles, but with a difference—they used them to sheath their designs.

Wealthy clients found the idea attractive and a style was born. The first Shingle-style houses were rambling two- or three-story structures; wooden shingles covered all exterior surfaces.

THREE-IN-ONE DESIGN: Bert Remmel designed this American Foursquare on Alameda Avenue. His design has elements from the Colonial Revival, Craftsman and Shingle styles.

While not every house sided in shingles represents the Shingle style, many homes have classic Shingle-style characteristics — rambling floor plans, inviting porches, high gables and rustic informality and, of course, shingles.

"(Richardson, McKim and White) used natural colors and informal compositions to suggest the rustic homes of New England settlers," says Craven. Other architects, designers and builders followed suit and covered their creations with shingle—not painted, but stained a single color. In doing so they created what Craven calls a "uniform, unembellished surface that celebrated the purity of line"—a purity that counterbalanced all the Queen Anne style's extraneous detailing.

The style did, however, lean on other styles for its expression and the term "Shingle style" did not enter the architectural vocabulary until Yale professor of architecture Vincent Scully coined it in 1955. Scully also coined the term "Stick style" to describe the style that followed the Victorian-era Italianate style.

The Shingle style's dependence on other Victorian-era styles is particularly evident here in Alameda. For example, when Joseph Leonard built his mansion along San Francisco Bay in 1896, he clad his home with its Queen Anne-style towers in shingles. And 12 years later when Annie Rix Militz and Harriet Hale Rix developed their property at Grand Street and Alameda Avenue shingles were an integral part of their Tudor Revival church and American Foursquare home.

Alameda historian Woody Minor tells us that Joseph A. Leonard—whose company was in the midst of developing the surrounding area—turned to his head draftsman, C. H. Russell, to design his home. Russell created a home that is less ornate and more horizontal than the typical Queen Anne-style house. Russell's plans included several striking aspects found in a Shingle-style residence: Unpainted wood shingles cover the entire exterior. Rugged stone defines the foundation and contrasts well with the shingles.

Rather then bedecking Leonard's Queen Anne-style home with its gingerbread, Russell starkly limited the home's exterior ornamentation. In so doing he integrated the towers and balcony with the rest of the home rather than setting them apart. Leonard's home included one feature of the Shingle-style home that was later removed: a prominent steeply pitched roof.

Two more examples of how builders integrated shingles into their designs can be see at the intersection of Grand Street and Alameda Avenue. In 1905 Julius Remmel's brother, Bert Remmel, designed the home at 1709 Alameda Avenue for Annie Rix Militz and Harriet Hale Rix. The sisters employed Remmel to design both their home and the Home of Truth sanctuary next door on Grand Street.

Remmel's design is an interesting blend of an American Foursquare home—the kind many less affluent Americans could order from a Sears catalog—with a Colonial Revival dormer looking from the roof onto the street. Remmel also poked the rafters out below the roofline, a nod to the Craftsman style, and added shingles to the home's architectural palette.

The sisters also turned to Bert Remmel to design the Tudor Revival sanctuary next door at 1300 Grand Street. He repeated the theme he used on the residence next door, mixing design elements that include the Tudor Revival exposed beams—and, of course, shingles.

Details, details!

Shingle style

HERE'S WHAT TO LOOK FOR:

1. Wavy and patterned wood shingles covering the siding and roof

2. An irregular roof line

3. Porches

4. Asymmetrical floor plans

5. Palladian windows, a large center window flanked by two smaller windows

6. Rough-hewn stone on lower stories with stone arches over windows and porches

THERE WERE NO RULE BOOKS. Not all Shingle-style homes have all the elements noted here. This Gold Coast home raises the question: Is this a Shingle-style home or a Queen Anne-style home with shingles?

THE AUTOMOBILE was considered a novelty in 1913 when Edward and Vernal Stang built this home on Eighth Street. It did not include the garage, which was added nine years later. Palm trees line Burbank Street in the background. This home is part of the Burbank-Portola Heritage Area, home to some of Alameda's more impressive Craftsman-style bungalows.

The Craftsman style

When the Arts and Crafts movement arrived in the United States the curtain had already begun to fall on the Victorian era. Just four years before Queen Victoria's death, a pair of exhibitions that heralded a design reform emphasizing craftsmanship and handicraft opened in Boston. This reform encouraged originality and the use of local materials. The exhibitions included hand-crafted furniture, jewelry, lamps, metalwork, pottery, tile, textiles and wallpaper.

A group of New England architects and designers opened 1897 with a January 4 exhibition at Boston's Museum of Fine Arts. They hoped to bring Britain's Arts and Crafts Movement to America; they succeeded. With this movement, the British had rebelled against late Victorian-era excess and a perceived disregard for the common worker.

Two months later, on April 5, the first American Arts and Crafts exhibition opened at Boston's Copley Hall. This exhibition showcased more than 1,000 objects made by 160 craftsmen, half of whom were women. The exhibition's success led to the June 28 incorporation of the Society of Arts and Crafts.

This society brought designers and workers together into mutually helpful relationships, worked to promote artistic work in all branches of handicraft and encouraged workers to execute their own designs.

ALAMEDA BUILDER R. C. Hillen sent postcards to renters promising he could build them a home just like the one pictured at the right for $2,900. He said he could offer "terms less than rent."

A style was born from this movement—one with simple, elegant designs that featured locally handcrafted wood, glass and metal work. As a reaction to Victorian-era opulence and the increasingly common mass-produced housing elements, the style—whose name comes from Gustav Stickley's popular magazine, *The Craftsman*—incorporated clean lines, sturdy structure and natural materials.

Many designers no longer looked to England, but found inspiration at home in sources like Shaker furniture. The style translated nicely from the simple to the complex; from furniture design to home design.

The masters

Charles and Henry Greene mastered the new design. "They developed a style of residential wooden buildings based entirely on craftsmanship principles," says Lester Walker in *American Homes*. The Greene brothers' best-known creation is the Gamble House in Pasadena. They designed both the house

Majestic palm trees set off a trio of West End streets that any Craftsman-style aficionado must visit: Burbank Street, Eighth Street and Portola Avenue. Together they form the Burbank-Portola Heritage Area.

and its furnishings in 1908 for David and Mary Gamble of the Procter and Gamble Company. The brothers built the Thorsen House on Berkeley's Piedmont Avenue the following year.

Alameda boasts a Craftsman-style jewel of its own. In 1908, Danish immigrant James Hansen Hjul designed and built an impressive home for himself and wife, Emma, on Grand Street.

Hjul was the founder of the J.H. Construction Company with offices in San Francisco's Mechanics Institute Building on Post Street. From 1907 to 1958 San Francisco city directories listed Hjul as a contractor, civil engineer, structural engineer and construction engineer. He did most of his work South of Market on warehouses and industrial buildings.

It's easy to spot a Craftsman-style home from the street. Handcrafted woodwork and stone serve as the first clues. Tapered square columns—with a front porch tucked neatly behind—support a low-pitched roof with overhanging eaves. Exposed rafters or decorative brackets complement the roof.

A must-see

Majestic palm trees mark a trio of West End streets that any aficionado of the Craftsman style must visit: Burbank Street, Eighth Street and Portola Avenue. Together they form the Burbank-

Portola Heritage Area, originally known as the Bay Park Tract. San Francisco investor John Dunn sold the property to the South Shore Land Company, which included William Farragut Chipman, the son of William Worthington Chipman, one of Alameda founders, and prominent lumberman Charles Hooper.

In 1909 the younger Chipman chose the names for the two new streets in the tract. He named one for the famous horticulturalist Luther Burbank. The year 1909 marked the 140th anniversary of Gaspar de Portola's discovery of San Francisco Bay, so William named the second new street Portola Avenue. Prospect Street, which already existed when the company laid out the tract, later underwent a name change to Eighth Street.

Sales got off to a slow start. William Thompson was the only taker in 1910. His house stood alone on today's Eighth Street until 1912 when the Stang brothers showed up. At first, Edward and Vernal Stang bought 16 lots in the tract. In the next three years the Stang Bros., as their firm was known, built 47 bungalows here, three-fourths of the 62 homes in the subdivision.

Historian Woody Minor describes the typical Stang bungalow in the Bay Park Tract as a 1,400 square-foot, two-bedroom, one-bath affair with a kitchen and breakfast nook.

In 1918 builder George Noble stepped in and built more homes in the tract. "His most telling change was in response to the automobile," Minor says. The tract's original improvements failed to include curb cuts for driveways.

Noble's homes here included a novelty not found in any of the Stang Bros. designs—garages. In one of Noble's 1925 homes it's interesting to note that the garage and the porch assume equal importance. By the time the Bay Shore Tract had seen its last home developed, the era of tract housing had been born and the automobile was here to stay.

Plan to stroll beneath the palms to enjoy the variety of Craftsman-style homes this heritage area has to offer.

Details, details!

Craftsman style

HERE'S WHAT TO LOOK FOR:

1. Hand-crafted woodwork and stone

2. A porch tucked behind tapered square columns

3. Low-pitched roof with overhanging eaves

4. Exposed rafters

THERE WERE NO RULE BOOKS and no mold for Craftsman-style houses. The oversized dormer on this home has lent it an unusual asymmetrical shape and added a comfortable second story.

BUNGALOW BLEND: This neat row of Mediterranean-style bungalows seems to lean toward the palm tree, giving this East End street an almost exotic atmosphere.

The Bungalow

The Bungalow

T he Victorian era left an impressive mark on Alameda's architectural landscape. Nineteenth-century gems shine on the city's Gold Coast. Architects and builders also scattered Victorian-era jewels in styles that range from the mid-19th century Gothic Revival to the early 20th-century Colonial Revival throughout Alameda.

Alameda is not just for aficionados of Victorian-era architecture, however. Another era left its mark here, one that appeared almost a quarter century after Queen Victoria's death—the Roaring '20s. This era brought prosperity to more than the upper crust and allowed those once not able to afford a home to live the American Dream.

The time was right to create a proper place for a type of home to fit this need in Alameda. In the fall of 1924 news reached Alamedans that Emilie Cohen had died on October 24. Emilie and Alfred A. Cohen had lived in their 50-room mansion on 106 acres on the city's East End they called "Fernside."

Creating a new Fernside

Alfred Cohen died in 1887. The mansion burned 10 years later on March 23, 1897, and the family moved into other buildings on the estate. When Emilie died, the children subdivided the estate and sold land to developers south of a boundary line that became Fernside Boulevard.

These developers created a neighborhood of homes each with their own personality; scarcely one is like the other. A red-tiled roof caps a Mediterranean-style home while half timbering defines the one next door as Tudor Revival. Exposed beams and hand-crafted shingles decorate a Craftsman-style home, while plaster covers the home next door emphasizing its simple lines.

A WIDE PORCH and overhanging eaves define this bungalow as one built in the Craftsman style.

I don't think the bungalow is a style. Rather, it is combination of design elements—the porch with its stoop and the low-pitched roof among them—that give styles like Tudor Revival, Craftsman and Mediterranean fresher, simpler more affordable personalities.

If you take a closer look something becomes apparent. It seems that most of these Fernside homes have elements in common.

It sets off one of those "ah-ha" moments when you realize it. Most of these homes are only one story (maybe a dormer protrudes from the roof above the entryway to create second "half story.") And most have porches and stoops. These are design elements that define a home—no matter its style—as a bungalow.

Defining a bungalow

What is a bungalow? I don't think the bungalow is a style. Rather, it is combination of design elements—the porch with its stoop and the low-pitched roof among them—that give styles like Tudor Revival, Craftsman and Mediterranean fresher, simpler, more affordable personalities.

In January 1913 *Sunset Magazine* offered this definition: "When you see a cozy one-storied dwelling, with low-pitched roof and very wide eaves, lots of windows and an outside chimney of cobble or clinker-brick half hidden by clinging vines—that is a bungalow, whatever other houses may be."

Writer and bungalow expert Jane Powell says that, "A bungalow is a one or one-and-a-half story house of simple design, expressed structure, built from natural or local materials, with a low-sloped roof, overhanging eaves and a prominent porch."

In the 'Bangla' style

The bungalow has its roots in the native architectural style of Bengal, India. English officers stationed there had small houses built in the "Bangla" style: one-story affairs with tile or thatched roofs and wide, covered verandas. They copied houses they saw used as rest houses for travelers, so the association was created early on that these were small houses for a temporary retreat.

PLASTER AND GEOMETRIC elements give this Alameda bungalow a crisp Art Deco personality.

Gustav Stickley gave the bungalow a pitch in an article he wrote in 1906. "Possibilities of the Bungalow as a Permanent Dwelling." Stickley's article led to the acceptance of the bungalow not just as a retreat but as a home.

While smaller and simpler than its bigger brothers and sisters found on the Gold Coast, Fernside bungalows display a wide palette of the various styles on the exterior, but especially on the interior where walls have elements like wainscoting and stenciling. Beamed ceilings set off the living and dining rooms. Tile and stone complement the floors.

Special places

The kitchen and the dining room played a special role in the creation of a bungalow's indoor spaces. "Unlike today, meals were eaten in the dining room," says Powell. This room "usually had a built-in china cabinet, as well as paneling and a plate rail for displaying plates and other artful objects."

And the meal? "The food came from the first truly modern kitchens," she says. "Indoor plumbing, electric lighting, gas stoves, and refrigeration, some of the better products of the Industrial Revolution, first came together in the kitchens of the Arts and Crafts era."

Built-in shelves or hutches abound and details like mullioned doors and beveled glass add grace and charm. Most homes boast a stone or brick fireplace with wood molding on the sides, a mantel above and decorative tile around the edges.

Built-in benches and breakfast nooks bring the Craftsman style indoors. An overabundance of windows allows natural light to shine into a home that almost anyone could afford in the era before the coming of the Great Depression.

Of course bungalows can be found throughout Alameda, but especially on Island City's East End where the neighborhood echoes the name, Fernside.

Have you ever noticed?

Alameda's architectural styles give many of the city streets their own personalities. This is particulary true of the streets in and around Fernside. A stroll down Thompson Avenue (which everybody knows is really called "Christmas Tree Lane") between High Street and Fernside Boulevard reveals a myriad of bungalows in different architectural styles. Just one block away on Liberty Avenue, the explorer will find every single bungalow in the Craftsman style. The bungalows on the streets to the west of High Street take on a more whimsical nature, echoing what some call the "Hansel and Gretel" style.

THE RED TILE ROOF and plaster leave no doubt that this bungalow was built in the Mediterranean Style.

Right in style

THE CRAFTSMAN-STYLE bungalow on page 101 and the one in the Mediterrean-style on page 103 were not the only ways to dress a bungalow. Builders clothed them in other styles popular in the late 19th and early 20th centuries. The dormer and bay window on the home seen above recall the Colonial Revival style. Half timbering dresses the gables on the bungalow shown above right, recalling the Tudor Revival style. Some bungalows have a certain whimsy about them. You'd almost expect Hansel or Gretel or Snow White to answer the door at the home on the right.

 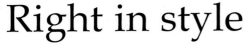

Details, details!

The Bungalow

HERE'S WHAT TO LOOK FOR:

1. Simple, modest scale

2. One or one-and-a-half stories tall

3. Low-pitched gable roofs

4. Front porch recessed under the main roof

5. Roofs with deep eaves

6. Exterior walls covered with shingles, clapboards, brick or stucco.

7. Materials applied in a simple rectilinear manner in contrast to the decorative Victorian-era styles

THERE WERE NO RULE BOOKS. Not all bungalows had all the elements noted here. For example, the house pictured here has a flat rather than an eaved roof.

TAKE A WALK THROUGH HISTORY at the Alameda Museum, which offers permanent displays of Alameda history, a rotating gallery showcasing local Alameda artists and student artwork, as well as souvenirs, books and videos about Alameda's history.

Epilogue

Preserving our heritage

We must all understand the profound importance of preserving Alameda's past. Start by getting to know more about Alameda's history first-hand at the Alameda Museum. Then support the museum with your membership and your involvement.

The Alameda Museum had its beginnings with the founding of the Alameda Historical Society in 1948. The society established the museum three years later. In 1983 the museum became the official repository of historical documents and artifacts for the City of Alameda.

Over the years the folks at the Alameda Museum have provided the city with a valuable service: preserving, interpreting and displaying evidence of Alameda's past. A dedicated group of volunteers continues this tradition.

You can also help preserve Alameda's architectural heritage by joining and supporting the Alameda Architectural Preservation Society.

While writing this book I decided to use a photograph from the Alameda Museum collection on the "Details, details" page in the Italianate chapter. I then discovered that had it not been for Pat Payne's very fiesty preservation efforts, Alameda would have lost this precious part of its heritage.

THIS HOME on Alameda Avenue was built on Santa Clara Avenue in the Italianate style in 1873 and moved to its present location in 1902. (See an earlier photograph of the home on page 63.)

Pat Payne owns the 1873 Italianate-style home that was built on the present site of Stone's Cyclery on Santa Clara Avenue near Park Street. In 1902 workers raised the structure off its foundation and placed it on rollers. A team of horses pulled the home to its present location on Alameda Avenue. Sometime in the 1930s, the owners removed the Italianate false front and remodeled the Italianate into the gable-roofed shingled home pictured on the preceding page.

In September 2000, neighbors awoke Pat with the frightening news that her house was on fire. After assessing the reality that the fire and ensuing water damage had completely ruined the home, Pat decided not just to repair the home, but to restore it to its Italianate splendor.

The Alameda Architectural Preservation Society honored Pat with a Historic Preservation Award in 2002.

According to the AAPS, Pat did not simply turn the restoration work over to others. She gave up her job and dedicated two years of her life "24 hours a day, seven days a week."

As just one part of the effort, Pat had to fight with her insurance company to force it to replace the home's damaged redwood with redwood instead of the plywood the insurer wanted to use. The final result of Pat's diligence is pictured on the left.

In a time when some in the city government look to save money by cutting the Alameda Museum's subsidy or by considering selling the Myers House and Garden to the Meyers Trust, which would sell it at no profit to the city, we should all show as much respect for our heritage as Pat Payne has done. It's time we all got involved in preserving Alameda's architectural treasure chest.

SPLENDID! Pat Payne's restoration work returned her home to its former Italianate glory. See the "before" photograph on the preceding page and an earlier photograph of the home on page 63.

The Alameda Museum

Anyone interested in informally learning about Alameda's history can visit the Alameda Museum at no cost. Visitors can browse through the Island City's past viewing exhibits, such as a facsimile of the barber shop where the city's beloved three-term Mayor Chuck Corica plied his trade and his grassroots politics.

Museum curator George Gunn and the museum board of directors also invite visitors to take in the museum's unique "annex" on Alameda Avenue, the Colonial Revival Meyers House and Gardens. There, for a small admission fee, visitors can immerse themselves in life in Alameda more than 100 years ago.

The museum also encourages local artists to display their work on its gallery walls, hosts a lecture series that focuses on Alameda's history, preserves hundreds and hundreds of documents and vintage photos, keeps a tangible array of Alameda's past and hosts special exhibitions that are lovingly put together by volunteers.

One of the best ways to support Alameda's heritage is with a membership in the Alameda Museum. Learn more at www.alamedamuseum.org or by calling (510) 521-1233.

THE ALAMEDA MUSEUM is located at 2324 Alameda Avenue near Park Street. Call ahead to check opening times. Admission is free.

Alameda Architectural Preservation Society

You are invited to become a member of the Alameda Architectural Preservation Society. To learn more, visit www.alameda-preservation.org.

The Alameda Architectural Preservation Society (AAPS) was founded as the Alameda Victorian Preservation Society in 1972 to preserve one of the finest and most concentrated collections of historical architectural styles left in the Bay Area.

Originally founded to save Victorian-era homes from being demolished and replaced with multi-unit housing, AAPS began helping owners of older buildings improve their properties without eroding Alameda's architectural character. The society also includes involvement with city government, historic home tours and public-service presentations on a wide variety of topics from lead paint abatement to Victorian-era wallpaper. Presentations are open to the public.

Expansion and alteration of older structures is sometimes required to accommodate modern living needs. These renovations may compromise the architectural integrity of historic buildings and surrounding neighborhoods. AAPS is available to assist businesses and homeowners in accomplishing their goals while preserving the original character of the building.

The *Alameda Sun* newspaper helps provide outreach for AAPS by featuring "Preservation Points" throughout the year. The column discusses the problems involved in maintaining or renovating an older building and present possible solutions that preserve architectural integrity. Topics include:

- Required permits by the City of Alameda
- Resources for historic preservation
- Hints on do-it-yourself projects
- Stories about restoration projects
- Questions and answers on historic preservation

There is no better way to support the AAPS than becoming a member. To learn more, visit the AAPS Web site at www.alameda-preservation.org, call (510) 986-9232 or drop them a line at AAPS, P.O. Box 1677, Alameda, CA 94501.

Bibliography

Books

A Diary from Dixie, Mary Boyton Chestnut

A Field Guide to American Houses, Virginia and Lee McAlester

A Living Legacy, Historic Architecture of the East Bay, Mark Wilson

Alameda: A Geographical History, Imelda Merlin

Alameda At Play, Woodruff Minor, Alameda Recreation and Park Department

A Treatise on the Theory and Practice of Landscape Gardening, A. J. Downing

A Pictorial Life of Jack London, Russ Kingman, Yukon Books

Burbank-Portola Heritage Area, Woodruff Minor

Cottage Residences, A.J. Downing and A.J. Davis

Documentation of Victorian and Post-Victorian Residential and Commercial Buildings City of Alameda 1854 to 1904, George C. Gunn

Expedition to San Francisco Bay in 1770: Diary of Pedro Fages, Herbert Bolton, editor, University of California Press

Fray Juan Crespi's Diaries, Herbert Bolton, editor, University of California Press

Gothic Revival, Megan Aldrich

Hints on Household Taste in Furniture, Upholstery and Other Details, Charles Eastlake

History of Alameda County, M. W. Wood 1883; reprint, Holmes Book Company

Rural Cottages, A.J Downing and A.J. Davis

Taking Care of Business: Historic Commercial Buildings of the Island City, Woodruff Minor, Alameda Museum

The Anza Expedition of 1775-1776: Diary of Pedro Font, Frederick Teggart, editor, University of California Press

The Cottage Souvenir Book, Revised and Enlarged, George F. Barber

The Architecture of Country Houses, A.J. Downing

Two Years Before the Mast, Richard Henry Dana

Ultimate Victorians, Elinor Richey

West Coast Victorians, A Nineteenth Century Legacy, Kenneth Naverson

Census pages

1850, 1860, 1870 census pages from www.ancestry.com

1852 California census, California State Library, Sacramento

Newspapers

Alameda Journal at Alameda Museum by Woodruff Minor

Alameda Semi-Weekly Argus newspaper articles at Alameda Museum

MacArthur Metro, Eleanor Dunn, *Shellmounds at the Base of Sausal Creek,* May 2003

New York Times, March 27, 1897, article about fire at Fernside

San Francisco Chronicle, David L. Baker, October 20, 2004, *On the Trail of Black Gold* article about ChrevonTexaco

Web sites

Alameda Museum, www.alamedamuseum.org

Alameda Architectural Preservation Society, www.alameda-preservation.org

Benicia State Capitol, www.parks.ca.gov/Default.asp?page_id=475

California brick-making, *calbricks.netfirms.com,* Dan Mosier

Cohen-Bray House, www.cohen-brayhouse.info

Gary Lenhart's Web site: www.alamedainfo.com

Michael Colbruno's Mountain View Cemetery blog, www.mountainviewpeople.blogspot.com

Pardee Home Museum, www.pardeehome.org

Vallejo home *Lachryma Montis,* www.parks.ca.gov/default.asp?page_id=22773

Maps

1875 Map of Alameda County, Oakland History Room

1888 *Alameda Semi-Weekly Argus* Map, Alameda Museum

1908 George Cram map from www.alamedainfo.com

Photo credits

Cover photo: Central Avenue about 1900, Alameda Museum

Inside front and back covers: 1878 Thompson & West maps, Oakland Public Library, Oakland History Room

Title page: August R. Denke, Alameda Museum

Facing page 1: *Alameda Semi-Weekly Argus* map, Alameda Museum

Page 1: Eli Dunning home, Alameda Museum

Page 2: Albert A. Hibbard home, Alameda Museum

Page 3: Benicia State Capitol Building, author

Page 4: Excavating the Sather Mound, Alameda Museum

Pages 5 and 6: Sather Mound artifacts, author

Page 7: Sather Mound hiking maps, Eric J. Kos

Page 8: Calendar panel, Peralta Hacienda Park

Page 9: Pedro Font map, Oakland Public Library, Oakland History Room

Page 10: 1852 Bolsa de Encinal, Oakland Public Library, Oakland History Room

Page 11: Alameda map, Alameda Museum

Page 12: Depassier, Maitre home, Alameda Museum

Page 14: Chipman photograph, Alameda Museum; Aughingbaugh grave marker, author

Page 15: Large map, Oakland Public Library, Oakland History Room; small map, Alameda Museum

Page 16: Town of Alameda map, Eric J. Kos

Page 17: George Cram map, Gary Lenhart

Page 20: Cyrus Wilson School, Gary Lenhart

Page 22: *Alameda Semi-Weekly Argus* map, Alameda Museum

Page 23: Large map, Oakland Public Library, Oakland History Room; small map, Alameda Museum

Page 24: Town of Encinal and Lands Adjacent map, Eric J. Kos

Page 26: Eagle Avenue remnant of Fassking's Park & Hotel, author

Page 27: String of Pearls, author

Page 29: Willow Street Queen Anne, author

Page 30: San Francisco & Alameda Railroad car barn, Alameda Museum

Page 31: Large map, Oakland Public Library, Oakland History Room; small map, Alameda Museum

Page 32: Town of Woodstock map, Eric J. Kos

Page 33: *Alameda Semi-Weekly Argus* map, Alameda Museum

Page 34: Kohlmoos Hotel, Alameda Museum; Blenheim Castle, private collection

Page 35: John London and Flora Wellman; Mountain View Cemetery; *Alameda Semi-Weekly Argus* map, Alameda Museum

Page 37: Pacific Coast Oil Works, Alameda Museum

Page 38: Oakland Public Library, Oakland History Room

Page 39: Henry and Ann Haight home, Alameda Museum

Page 40: Dr. William Lum's Tudor Revival home, author

Page 42: A. J. Downing and A. J. Davis photos, private collection

Page 43: Gothic-style house from A. J. Downing's *Rural Cottages*, private collection

Page 44: Webster House, author

Page 45: Rich family house, author

Page 47: *Lachryma Montis*, Daniella Thompson

Page 48: J. Moss Mora home, private collection

Page 49: Braced-frame house, private collection

Page 51: Balloon-frame house, private collection

Page 52: Franklin Pancoast home, author

Page 53: D. L. Munson home, author

Page 54: M. F. Bishop home, author

Page 55: Pardee home, Oakland Public Library, Oakland History Room

Page 57: Thompson & West map, Oakland Public Library, Oakland History Room; hiking map, Eric J. Kos

Page 58: *Alameda Semi-Weekly Argus* map, Alameda Museum

Page 59: Jack Hays, Mountain View Cemetery

Page 60: Eadward Muybridge photograph of Fernside, California Views Historical Photo Collection

Page 61: A. A. Cohen, Cohen-Bray House

Page 63: Alameda Avenue Italianate, Alameda Museum

Page 64: Croll's, Alameda Museum

Page 65: Britt Hotel, Alameda Museum

Page 66: *Alameda Semi-Weekly Argus* map, Alameda Museum

Page 67: Edward Childs' home, author

Page 68: Old Governor's Mansion, Mary Stuart Gillian

Page 69: Julius Remmel home, author

Page 70: Pollen Cunningham home, author

Page 71: George A. Bordwell home, author

Page 72: Pair of Park Avenue Stick-style cottages, author

Page 73: Robert Harvey home, author

Page 74: Cohen-Bray House, author

Page 75: Willow Street Stick-style house, Alameda Museum

Page 76: Walter W. Haskell house, author

Page 77: Alonzo Fink house, author

Page 78: Corliss engine, private collection

Page 79: Dutch India ship *Amsterdam*, Jessica and Eric on Flickr

Page 80: Gilded sunburst, author

Page 81: David Brehaut house, author; George S. Barber Design 27, private collection

Page 82: David Brehaut house gingerbread, author

Page 83: Scroll Saw No. 7, private collection

Page 85: Queen Anne house, Alameda Museum

Page 86: Garratt Mansion, author

Page 88: Joseph and Teresa Mallon home, author

Page 89: Henry H. Meyers house, author

Page 90: Colonial Revival-style homes on Everett Street, author

Page 91: Colonial Revival house, Alameda Museum

Page 92: Joseph Leonard house, author

Page 93: Rix family house, author

Page 95: Gold Coast Shingle-style house, author

Page 96: Stang Bros. cottage, author

Page 97: R. C. Hillen creation on Liberty Avenue, Gary Lenhart

Page 99: Craftsman-style home on Fernside Boulevard, author

Page 100: "Bungalow Blend," author

Page 101: Craftsman-style bungalow, author

Page 102: Art Deco bungalow, author

Page 103: Mediterranean-style bungalow, author

Page 104: A trio of bungalows, all by the author

Page 105: Fernside bungalow, author

Page 106: Alameda Museum showcases, Alameda Museum

Page 107: 2121 Alameda Avenue before, Alameda Museum

Page 108: 2121 Alameda Avenue after, Alameda Museum

Page 109: Alameda Museum, author

Index